THE FULL MOON YEARBOOK

A year of ritual and healing
under the light of the full moon

Julie Peters

Illustrated by
Lauren Spooner

DAVID & CHARLES

www.davidandcharles.com

CONTENTS

INTRODUCTION

A LITTLE ABOUT ME

I have loved the moon for as long as I can remember. I would watch it shift and change outside my window at night, talk to it when I was out with my dog after dark, pray to it when I felt lost. I remember one night on a long road trip with my brother, camping somewhere in eastern Canada in a tent with a skylight, waking up with a start to see the eyeball of the full moon staring straight down at me. Years later, I would wake my lover at all hours of the night when there was a lunar eclipse and drive to the beach to watch it turn red. In 2016, I wrote a book on a set of Tantric moon phase goddesses called the Nityas who changed my relationship with the moon as well as with myself. I have been a moon lover—a lunatic—for a long time.

The moon holds its own special magic, and there has been mythology and meaning to the moon in pretty much every culture in every era throughout the world. A common prayer in Irish folklore when one first noticed the moon was "God bless the Moon and God bless me, I see the moon and the moon sees me." There's something about the moon that makes us feel as if we are in a relationship with it, as if it looks back at us, following our gaze through the car window even as we zip along the highway.

My ancestors are from England and Ireland, where ancient religions knew to follow the moon and the seasons carefully and celebrate the changes of the Wheel of the Year. I was born as a fourth-generation Canadian in Ontario, on Mississauga, Anishnabeg, and Haudenosaunee land (among others), near the Great Lakes, with its wet snow in the winter and the persistent, insistent mosquitoes in the summer. I now live in Edmonton, Alberta, a northern prairie city where the sun sets at 4:00 pm in the winter and the air gets so cold sometimes it literally sparkles. As I write this, I am on Plains Cree land on Treaty 6 territory, an area known as Amiskwaciy Waskahikan. My work with the moon isn't just about the moon, it's also about the seasons, the weather, the trees, my place here, my family's history, and my intention to learn, understand, and heal.

LAND ACKNOWLEDGMENTS

In the ritual sections of each month, I will ask you to take a moment to consider the land that you are on and your relationship with that land. Here in Canada, it has become more common for speakers at events, for example, to do a land acknowledgment before they begin; that is, they name the traditional territories they are on and the people who were here first. It is a gesture of respect and remembrance for the First Peoples and First Nations of this place and a step toward reconciliation after the many wounds caused by colonization.

Land acknowledgments can also help us think about our individual, personal, intimate relationship with the land, which is partly what the full moons of the year can teach us. I can consider where my family came from. I can also consider how the local flora and fauna make me feel in my body, how the phase of the moon pulls on my dreams, and the quality of the light behind my eyes.

As we explore each month's lunation and how it connects to the season, we are necessarily considering the land. I encourage you to do a land acknowledgment no matter where you and your ancestors are from. Consider your relationship with the natural world around you as you get to know the moons, the seasons, and your own relationship with the land.

SCIENTIFIC MOON MAGIC

The moon has a few fascinating qualities, and one of them is that we all see the same moon phase and moon face, no matter where we are in the world. In a poetic cosmic coincidence, the moon's spin perfectly matches that of the earth, so even though the moon does shift and change, it only ever shows us the same face.

This is a phenomenon called geosynchronous orbit. Because the moon has no atmosphere, its surface rarely changes, so the shadows and pits we can see from earth never change. In addition, the timing of the moon's movement around the earth (which takes a month) and the spin of the earth around itself (which takes a day) means that everywhere in the world, we experience the same moon phase. A full moon in China is a full moon in the southern USA. As different as our experiences of the land may be, the moon brings us all back together. No matter who we are or where we live, we all share the same moon.

The earth and the moon have a gravitational connection. They pull on each other just a little bit, which affects the shape of the fluid oceans as we spin. Full moons happen when the earth, sun, and moon line up, with the moon located on the far side of the earth, where it is fully illuminated by the sun. New moons create the same kind of gravitational pull, but the moon is between the sun and the earth, bringing it fully into shadow. During the half moons, the position of the moon is perpendicular to the earth relative to the sun, so the energies are more balanced.

Think of the earth as a liquidy blob (which it is, sort of), with the sun and moon pulling gently on the ocean. High tides happen when the water is being pulled toward the moon, and low tides happen when that coast is perpendicular to the moon. During full and new moons, the alignment of the three bodies creates a higher gravitational pull, causing the tides to be more dramatic. High tides during this time are called Spring tides. During the first and last quarter moons, when the sun and moon are at right angles to each other, their gravitational pull balances, creating more moderate tides known as Neap tides.

There aren't really any studies on how the tides and the pull of the moon may affect our bodies, and most scientists think it's likely too subtle of an effect for us to notice. But many of us can feel the moons anyway, noticing more intensity of emotions or dreams around the full and new moons and more balanced energies around the quarter phases. The menstrual cycle has long been associated with the moon phases, as it's intuitive that a monthly cycle that pulls the tides might also affect the flow inside of our bodies. Perhaps these effects are too subtle and layered to be studied in a lab, but that doesn't mean they aren't real. Getting to know your body in relationship to the year's moons may give you some information about your own subtle inner cycles as we flow through the Wheel of the Year. You know your body better than anyone else: trust your intuition.

ON THE FULL MOON NAMES

The moon has been a tool for keeping time and seasons for cultures all over the world as long as people have been around. The word "moon" is etymologically linked to the word for "month," from the Greek *mēn* and Latin *mensis*, which is also where we get our word for menstruation.

Before the modern calendar year, cultures all over the world tracked the seasons using lunations. Our Gregorian calendar splits the year up into twelve months in order to stay in alignment with the solar year. These months were mostly named by the Roman ruler Julius Caesar, and follow the rhythms of war. The year began in March, a month named for the war god Mars, which was when it warmed up enough for the soldiers to get back to the work of fighting. The period between December and March didn't get named, at first, because it was too cold and dark to do much of anything.

Most of the world follows this modern calendar, but there are still names for each moon that are relevant in traditional societies everywhere. There are ancient Celtic names for the moon from Europe, colonial American names developed by the settlers living on the land, Chinese names, Wiccan and Neo-Pagan names, and various names from Indigenous communities. In this book, we are working with names from the Northern Hemisphere. There are, of course, plenty of different moon names in the Southern Hemisphere, but the seasons would be reversed and the seasonal stories would have their own resonances with the rhythms of those lands.

While a modern calendar month is an average of 30.4 days, a moon cycle is only 29.5 days, so of course the moon cycles don't exactly match our months as we know them. Some years have thirteen full moons within them, and that extra full moon would be called a blue moon. The full moon names we're working with here will wobble around the months as they are more connected to seasonal changes than specific calendar dates.

In this book, I have collected as many names for the moon as I could, but as I've come to realize, they are likely countless. The names offered by the *Old Farmer's Almanac* are the ones that are most commonly cited, based on the discoveries of Jonathan Carver, who traveled among the Dakota Sioux of North America. However, plenty of this full moon knowledge is highly local and often passed down orally, held in local communities rather than in reference books. Despite that, however, many of the moon names have something in common as they express the general energy of that time of year. I chose the full moon name for each month that resonates the most with the general energies of that period of time as I understand them. You may have a different experience, so feel free to look through the alternative moon names and see if anything there resonates more deeply with you. Similarly, feel free to pick and choose from the rituals and suggestions that you're interested in, and leave whatever doesn't work for you right now.

A NOTE ON THE YOGA

Each lunation has a yoga pose that resonates with the energy of that time of year. Most of the poses can be done on their own unless otherwise indicated, but if you have a regular yoga practice, you can also simply incorporate that pose into your routine. None of the yoga poses should hurt, and if anything doesn't feel right for you, stop right away. Check with your health practitioner before doing these poses to ensure they are safe and right for you.

At the end of this book, you'll also find the yoga poses linked together as a full Wheel of the Year sequence that you can do anytime, as well as a Moon Salutation practice that might be especially suited to the full moon phase. Here, too, modify as you need to and avoid anything that causes pain.

JANUARY

WOLF MOON

Names of the Moon

English Medieval: Wolf Moon

Wiccan: Wolf Moon

Celtic: Quiet Moon

Cherokee: Cold Moon

Dakota Sioux: Moon of the Terrible

Colonial American: Winter Moon

Anishinaabe: Spirit Moon

Cree: Frost Exploding Moon

Chinese: Holiday Moon

European: Moon After Yule

Roman: Janus, God of Doorways

HOWLING IN THE DARK

The January full moon is cold and clear, dark and still. We've just moved past the winter solstice, so we are technically on the other side of the darkening year, but we are still very much with the long, cold nights. I've been known to spend my afternoons sun-chasing with my dog, trying (and failing) to find pockets of sunshine, already hidden by long shadows at three in the afternoon, the sun circling low, the sun and I both thinking about going back to bed.

January was decreed to be the first month of the year by the Roman emperor Julius Caesar, who eventually named this month after Janus, a god of doorways and new beginnings. Janus has two faces, one looking forward and one looking back, so he represents the shift from one state to another. The New Year's Resolutions tradition dates back to Babylonian times, and cultures all over the world will tend to have a moment of reflection and resolution on the New Year (which may land in spring, fall, or elsewhere, depending on whom you ask). Common intentions to lose weight and exercise more likely come from colonial Protestants who valued a strong work ethic, religious consistency, and restraint around pleasure.

Resolving to change everything in early January is a difficult task indeed: there is so little energy coming from the sun that our bodies will tend to resist, especially if our resolutions involve things like more exercise or eating less.

The Dakota Sioux called this the Moon of the Terrible, and indeed this month can be. The harvest stores are getting thin and holiday celebrations are over. This month didn't even have a name in the original Roman calendar, it was a part of a sort of dead zone in the year when it was too cold to go to war, so people just took a break.

January is a common time for depression, especially after the rich holiday season, which is celebrated in some way in almost every culture and religion worldwide. December tends to be full of celebrating, spending, seeing family (or not), and gathering with friends (or not). January can feel like a spiritual hangover. Several communities think of this lunation as the Wolf Moon, where the wolves could be heard howling in the dark, cold nights.

Wolves howl for many reasons, but it was thought that they were howling because they were hungry. It feels right to howl at the moon (metaphorically, probably) from a place of deep hunger, whether that's for the light and nourishment of the withholding earth or for a genuine, warm connection with someone who loves us even when we are not at our bright and shiniest. This can be a month of loneliness.

As difficult as this time can feel, there are ways we can soften the sharpness of the Wolf Moon. The Celtic name for this lunation is the Quiet Moon, and it's prescriptive as much as it is descriptive. It's time to stay inside, to be quiet, to nourish ourselves with gentleness and warmth. There is an invitation to rest in the dark, here; not as a way to wallow in depression, for example, but rather as a way to remain in the dreamy, quiet mood of January's Wolf Moon, to trust that our inner howling will be met, in time, if we know how to honor its messages.

Someone I loved once gave me a box full of darkness. It took me years to understand that this, too, was a gift.

~ MARY OLIVER

SEASONAL WELLNESS

- Spend time in meditation or contemplation. Allow yourself to see what's present in the darkness of your mind. Imagine, intend, dream, and wish.

- Stay at home, in the quiet, and read or write, reflecting on the darker thoughts that may arise during this time. Say no if you don't feel like going out with friends.

- Write down your dreams.

- Eat warm, cooked foods, drink warm beverages, and spend time with a heating pad or hot water bottle on your mid-back, where your adrenal glands can get overly cold and depleted.

- Hot baths, saunas, and hot tubs can be a balm for those extra cold nights in this season.

- Practice gentle yoga and other forms of movement that aren't exhausting.

- Sleep. Naturally, our bodies want a longer night's rest when the light is lower. Go to bed earlier, wake up later, and nap, if you can.

- If you've made a New Year's Resolution, consider where that tradition comes from and why you feel you need to do it. Is your resolution aligning with what's best for you and your community? Or is it coming from a place of cultural pressure or even guilt?

- Spend time outside, when appropriate, if possible walking (or snowshoeing) in a quiet wood during the brightest part of the day.

- When it's dark, which it will be a lot, look out for the light of the moon.

JOURNAL PROMPT

What is revealed to me when I allow myself to see what's in the dark?

AFFIRMATION

Rest is my medicine.

THE FOUR OF SWORDS

Many tarot decks show this card with a person resting on something that looks a little like a coffin, with three swords hanging above them and one sword alongside them. There's a romance with death here, but not in a final way. It's a call for deep rest and contemplation. Swords represent the intellect and the element of air. This is often the most difficult suit of the deck because it has to do with the stories we tell ourselves, especially, in this case, the "shoulds" we get from our culture: we should lose weight, we should go running every day, we should be exactly as productive now as when there's twice the light in the sky. The person in the image is in a posture of sleep, but their thoughts are hanging over their head, preventing them from resting fully. Take your worries out and take a good look at them. How close are they to reality? Is the story you are telling about yourself the only possible story, or is there another way to tell that tale? How could you set those thoughts aside and allow your body to truly, deeply rest?

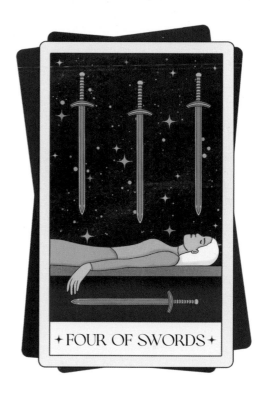

YOGA POSE

CHILD'S POSE

Child's Pose is a gentle shape that softly opens the back and hips. It is nourishing for our adrenal glands, which are located in the mid back just underneath the shoulder blades. This is where adrenaline and cortisol are produced, and this area can get overtaxed during the holidays and when we rush to get back to work in January. Gently opening and stretching this area can help to soothe stress in the body, which supports our immune system, hormones, digestion, sleep, and all kinds of other things.

To begin Child's Pose, come onto your hands and knees. Bring your big toes together and allow your knees to widen about hip-width apart, and feel free to adjust this according to your comfort level.

If you have a bolster or large cushion, place it between your knees and lie forward over your thighs. Rest your cheek on the cushion or your forehead on the floor or another prop if that's most comfortable.

Cover your lower and mid back with a blanket or a heating pad. You could also place a blanket or cushion between your hips and heels for more support. Rest for five to ten minutes or as long as you feel comfortable.

SPELL JAR RITUAL

January is not great for action, but it is a wonderful time for dreaming, feeling, wishing, and intending. Making a spell jar on the January full moon is a sweet practice that can be done with simple ingredients you have around the house. Start with a clean jar with a lid, some salt, and a candle.

Next, you'll gather your own special ingredients. As you consider what you want in the coming year, bring together simple household items to symbolize those desires. For example, honey could represent sweetness, a splash of whiskey or wine for pleasure, cayenne pepper for energy, or rose petals for grief support. You may have buttons, stones, crystals, or pieces of paper with your intentions written on them. There's no wrong thing to put in your spell jar, it simply needs to mean something to you.

Once you've gathered your ingredients, light your candle.

Visualize a circle of protection around yourself, perhaps made of salt or stones. Clarify that you are within a circle that only allows in energies that are supportive of your highest good, and anything else is filtered out.

Take a moment to acknowledge the land that you are on and your relationship with this land. You may also like to invite any energies that may be helpful for you in this ritual. This could include loved ones, pets, deities, spirit guides, the earth, the sky, the four directions, or whatever resonates for you.

Put a little bit of salt in the bottom of your spell jar, which provides cleansing and protection. Then add your ingredients one at a time, considering what they mean to you as you do.

When this feels complete to you, place the lid on the jar. You could use a little bit of candle wax to seal the lid closed. Thank your energies, the ingredients in your jar, the land, and anything else that you feel needs gratitude. Blow out your candle. Your ritual is complete. Keep the spell jar somewhere you're likely to look at it often.

ENERGIES OF THE MOON PHASES

Just as each full moon throughout the year has its own mood and energy, so does each phase of each lunation. As you're getting to know the year's moons, you may also want to look at how their phases feel in your body and in different seasons. Generally, the energies of the moon phases will be most intense for three days; for example, the day before, the day of, and the day after the full moon.

NEW MOON

During this phase, the moon is between the earth and the sun, which means its face is completely in shadow, so we can't see it at all. From our perspective, the moon appears to pause, to rest for a moment on its monthly journey. However, its gravitational pull is stronger because it is in alignment with the gravity of the sun, a cosmic phenomenon known as syzygy. We can feel an intensity around the new moon, but it is a mood of darkness and quiet. In general, this is a time to pause and reflect on intentions, wishes, dreams, and desires, but it's not time for action yet. There is a parallel here to the feel of the winter solstice season—November, December, and January— the darkest months of the year, when we are meant to be quiet, reflective, and sitting with our intentions rather than acting on them.

WAXING MOON AND THE FIRST QUARTER

The moon waxes between the new and full moon, gaining light and energy. The period before the first quarter, when the moon appears to be halved in the sky, is called a waxing crescent. The period after, when we are closer to the full moon, we have a waxing gibbous moon. Around the first quarter (the half moon), the moon is perpendicular to the earth in relation to the sun, so the gravitational pull is gentler than during the full or new moons. There is light in the sky, but it's not as overwhelming as it can be when the full moon appears. Right now the energies are balanced but growing, so this is an ideal time to take action. Start new projects, get to know new people, and nurture your creativity. The waxing moon parallels the spring season, from February through May or so, when the days are lengthening, warmth is growing, and the flowers begin to bloom.

FULL MOON

When the whole face of the moon is completely illuminated in a perfect circle, the moon is on the far side of the earth, with the sun's light shining on it completely. The gravitational pull on the oceans is similarly intense to that of the new moon phase (the alignment known as syzygy). It feels quite different, however, because of the full moon's intense illumination at night. It's common for the full moon to affect our sleep, giving us vivid dreams or keeping us awake all night. The full moon shines a light in the dark, which means emotions and memories that are normally hidden away can seem to rise from the deep, demanding our attention. The full moon can be energizing and powerful, but it can also hit a little too hard, nudging us over into stagnation or frustration. This is an important time to pause, but where the new moon invites us to consider our intentions, the full moon gives us an opportunity to let go, to release whatever is no longer serving us. This phase parallels the energy of the bright, hot, fun (but sometimes exhausting) summer solstice season in June, July, and August.

WANING MOON AND THE LAST QUARTER

The moon wanes between the full moon and the new moon, which means its light is diminishing. Just after the full moon, this is a waning gibbous moon, and closer to the new moon it is called a waning crescent moon. The last quarter (also called the third quarter; right between the full and new moon) feels very similar to the first quarter, as the moon is perpendicular to the earth with its more moderate gravitational pull, and looks identically halved in the sky. However, the light is diminishing rather than growing, and this phase is best for integrating and processing rather than building, as you might on the waxing moon. On the last days of the waning crescent, it's a good idea to clean up your house, organize your desk, and finish up anything you can in preparation for the pause and rest that's needed during the new moon. The waning moon phase parallels the withdrawing mood of the autumn equinox season, which happens around September and October.

FEBRUARY

BUDDING MOON

Names of the Moon

Chinese: Budding Moon

English Medieval: Storm Moon

Wiccan: Storm Moon

Celtic: Moon of Ice

Cherokee: Bony Moon

Dakota Sioux: Moon of the Raccoon,
Moon When the Trees Pop

Colonial American: Trapper's Moon

Anishinaabe: Bear Moon

Neo-Pagan: Snow Moon

American Indian: Snow Moon

Roman: Februalia

HOPE AFTER STRUGGLE

Several cultures refer to this month's lunation as the Snow Moon: a time when the world is buried under a bright blanket of snow. And of course in many parts of the Northern Hemisphere, we are essentially still in midwinter, with spring off in the distance of later March (if that). And yet, there is an energy of change just below the surface of that snow.

The Chinese name for this lunation is the Budding Moon, and this is the season of the Lunar New Year in China, Japan, Korea, Vietnam, and many other places in the East Asian cultural sphere. The celebrations usually begin on the second new moon after the winter solstice, which tends to land in late January or early February. This festival marks the beginning of spring, which may seem far off to many of us in the more northern regions of the world, but even in the frigid Snow Moon prairies, you can begin to feel the daylight stretching. This is a better time to think about new beginnings and new possibilities than during the forbidding January Wolf Moon. The sun's energy is making itself known again, even if the world feels buried in cold and snow.

The word for this month refers to an ancient Roman festival called Februalia from the Latin root word *februa* that means "to cleanse." This was a festival of purification and atonement before the new year began for the Romans in March.

Even in more northern climates, the first few days of February are celebrated as Imbolc, St. Brigid's Day, or Groundhog Day—all celebrations that mark the halfway point between the winter solstice and the spring equinox. Brigid was an ancient Celtic goddess of healing, fertility, magic, poetry, and domesticated animals. She is often shown carrying a bowl of fire, and represents the energy of early spring. It was traditionally a day for weather divination, and devotees of Punxsutawney Phil in the United States still celebrate Groundhog Day by watching to see if a small rodent can predict how much winter we've still got left to get through. This is a moment when we welcome the very earliest shifts from the dark season toward the warmth and abundance of the bright half of the year.

The Gaelic word *imbolc* may mean "in the belly," and likely references lambing season, a time when the lambs are being born and milk is forthcoming. This is a welcome gift when harvest stores from the fall have thinned. Another possible meaning of the word is "budding," which is also the Chinese name of this month's moon. Where I grew up, in southern Ontario, the idea of spring in February was a joke. But when I lived in Vancouver, I'd be shocked to walk outside on a cold, dark February morning and see tiny white snowdrops and fat rhododendron buds thirsty for sun, just thinking about opening up.

The energy of this month's lunation is spring fire alit beneath the snow. It is a reminder that the energy of change is coming, even if you can't quite see it yet. The shift into a brighter, warmer mood is delicate and subtle now, and you may feel it more or less depending on where you live. The intentions, dreams, and wishes you have been gestating since the winter solstice may now feel like they are ready to actually get started. As the light grows and the winds change, we may feel our spirits shifting in response, preparing to move out of the quiet contemplation of the winter season and into the bright half of the year—but not quite yet.

THE GODDESS BRIGID

The Celtic goddess Brigid, Christianized into St. Brigid, is a goddess of the eternal flame. She is a protector of women; it is said that the hedge around the sacred flame at St. Brigid's sanctuary at Kildare in Ireland could cause death or insanity to any man who tried to cross it. She is often shown carrying a bowl of fire and with a crown of bright red hair, sometimes with a field behind her, cows and ewes in the background, a handful of sunny yellow dandelions in her hand. Her fire not only warms the earth in preparation for spring, but also invites the energy of creativity, passion, and the magic of conception.

SEASONAL WELLNESS

- Take another look at your New Year's Resolutions or other plans or intentions you have been thinking about, and start taking the first steps toward making change.

- Spend time with fire, if you can: a fireplace, a candle, or a bonfire are all wonderful ways to honor Brigid, align with the new energy of the early spring, and welcome the Budding Moon.

- Nurture the buds of change within you. Don't try to do too much yet, but stay open to new possibilities as they come.

- This is a good time for cleansing, clearing, and decluttering.

- You may find yourself able to do a little bit more in terms of movement and getting outside. Find those rays of sun, if possible, and receive them.

- Cultivate the fire in your own belly by drinking ginger tea, adding warming spices like chili and cinnamon to your food, and eating bitter dandelion leaves, a flower sacred to the goddess Brigid.

- If there are any Lunar New Year celebrations in your area that you can attend, go and celebrate! See more on the Lunar New Year later in this month.

JOURNAL PROMPTS

How would you like to invite the energy of spring fire or the Lunar New Year into your life? What do you need to let go of in order to do this?

AFFIRMATION

I nourish the spark of passion in my belly.

THE STAR

The Star tarot card usually shows a young woman pouring a pitcher of water into a body of water and another onto the land. She is usually naked with a bright star above her head, rolling hills lush with green behind her. This scene echoes images of the goddess Brigid, bringing life back to the land with her sacred fire after the long winter. The Star appears after the Tower numerically in the tarot deck, and indicates hope after something really devastating has happened. The Star brings the delicate early spring energy of new life, new hope, and bright possibility after it feels as if everything has been lost. She is a reminder that new life always follows death, that possibility always returns, even when it feels like things have been really hard. This is the mood of this month's lunation, which is both the Snow Moon, where we are still reckoning with the reality of the winter, and the Budding Moon, where the earliest signs of new life become visible. This is a moment for hope.

YOGA POSE

SUN SALUTATION

A Sun Salutation is traditionally practiced to welcome the coming of the light. This is the perfect sequence to shake off the heaviness of the wintertime and invite the gentle shifting into light. This variation of Sun Salutation is appropriate for most bodies and activates most major muscle groups in the body.

Start by standing in Tadasana with your feet parallel, about hip-width apart, hands resting at your sides.

Inhale: Reach your arms up to the sky.

Exhale: Fold forward over your legs with your knees as bent as you need.

Inhale: Halfway Lift: reach your chest up, with your knees a bit bent, looking slightly forward, almost like a backbend.

Exhale: Step back to Downward Facing Dog. Your first finger should point forward with your arms a bit wider than shoulder-width apart. Bend your knees as much as you need to, and stretch your hips up and back.

Inhale: Plank Pose: bring your shoulders over your wrists. Engage your core and look slightly forward so that your spine is in a long line. Knees may be on the floor.

Exhale: Lower all the way to the ground.

Inhale: Cobra Pose: engage your legs, glutes, and core. Gently lift your chest up off the earth with very little weight on your hands.

Exhale: Press back to Downward Facing Dog.

Inhale: Reach your right leg up to the sky as high as feels good for you right now.

Exhale: Step your foot forward to your hands. You may need to grab the foot and step it forward to your hands. Lower your back knee to the floor (optional).

Inhale: Lunge: reach your arms up to the sky.

Exhale: Return to Downward Facing Dog.

Inhale: Reach your left leg up to the sky.

Exhale: Step your foot through and lower your back knee down (optional).

Inhale: Lunge: reach your arms up to the sky.

Exhale: Return to Downward Facing Dog. Inhale here.

Exhale: Step or jump your feet to your hands.

Inhale: Halfway Lift.

Exhale: Fold forward.

Inhale: Reach your arms up to the sky.

Exhale: Remain standing and bring your hands together to touch in front of your heart.

If you wish, repeat this sequence three times.

BUDDING MOON RITUAL

February is a time for early spring cleansing, especially in alignment with Februalia, the month–long Roman festival of cleansing, purification, and atonement in preparation for the new year beginning. Before you sit down for this simple ritual, spend some time clearing out your closet, cleaning your house, or tidying in whatever way resonates with you best. All you need for the ritual itself is a candle and a pen and paper.

Light your candle. Imagine your circle of protection that only allows in the energies that are in alignment with your highest good. Make your acknowledgment to the land. Close your eyes and consider what you are ready to sweep away from the dark winter season. As you imagine each thing, offer it into the candle flame, imagining it being incinerated, transformed by the fire, and released from your body.

You may also want to spend some time with atonement, considering any regrets, learnings, or apologies from the past year and offering them into the fire.

Next, consider your desires and goals over the next little while. Gently watch the candle flame and imagine drawing it into your belly, sparking your ability to go for it.

Write down your desires, goals, and the steps you will take to go toward what you want.

When this is complete for you, ritually cleanse your body with a shower, a bath, or simply by washing your hands mindfully, symbolically cleansing yourself in preparation for the new spring energy.

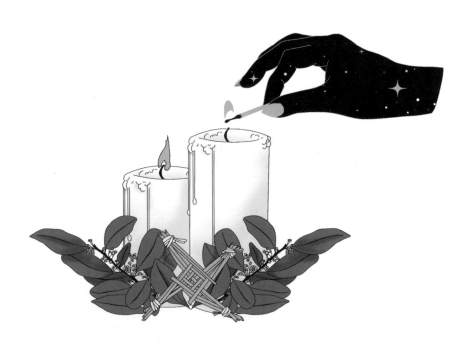

LUNAR NEW YEAR

The Lunar New Year is celebrated by many cultures in the East Asian cultural sphere. It falls on the first new moon of the Lunar year, which lands around the end of January or beginning of February, and it's the biggest time of year for families to travel to be together. This is the most important holiday of the year, and it lasts for a full waxing moon phase, the fifteen days or so from new moon to full moon.

Traditionally, the week before the festival involves lots of preparation, including spring cleaning. Houses are cleansed of any lingering bad luck, making space for good luck to come, a process called "sweeping of the grounds." Food is a central aspect of the festival, involving feasts of rice, moon cakes, dumplings, fish, and other special meals. Celebrants give each other red paper envelopes filled with money for good luck. The full moon at the end of the holiday usually comes with a Lantern Festival with parades, fireworks, colorful lanterns, and more.

One of the legends of the ancient roots of this festival is that a monster named Nian was threatening to eat everyone on the New Year's Day. On finding out that this creature feared the color red along with loud noises, the people had a festival with bright lanterns and red paper decorations all night long and successfully kept him away. From a seasonal perspective, we might think of that monster as the heavy and sometimes depressive energy that can weigh on us in December and January. Cleaning the house, celebrating with friends, feasting, and inviting the light to return with bright lights and loud noises can banish seasonal depression and help us shift our energy into the hopeful bright fire of the early spring and the Lunar New Year.

MARCH

WORM MOON

Names of the Moon

Dakota Sioux: Worm Moon

English Medieval: Chaste Moon

Wiccan: Chaste Moon

Celtic: Moon of Winds

Cherokee: Windy Moon

Colonial American: Fish Moon

Anishinaabe: Sugar Moon

Ojibwe: Sugar Moon

Chinese: Sleepy Moon

European: Lenten Moon

Neo-Pagan: Death Moon

Roman: Mars, God of War

UGLINESS BEFORE BEAUTY

March brings the spring equinox on or around March 21st. The darkness and daylight are roughly equal on the equinox, which marks the official beginning of spring. But depending on where you live, it may still feel very much like winter. Here in the northern prairies, March is the most frustrating month. You've been waiting for spring for so long, and when you go outside you're hit with cold winds, your boots still buried in feet of snow. In the city parks on the West Coast, on the other hand, the robins show up in March, pecking at the cold, wet earth, snacking on the worms who are having a party in the softening dirt. This is the Worm Moon, when the energy of spring wriggles up to the surface, even if that surface is still covered in snow.

The Worm Moon is likely named for the earthworms that tend to appear around this time, but it may also refer to the beetle larvae that begin to emerge from the tree bark, making the trees seem as if they are waking up, too, shaking off the cold of winter and shuddering back to life. It might be a bit of an ugly name, but the beginning of spring often is ugly—it's damp, it's weird, and there needs to be worms and larvae before there can be colorful blooms and soft breezes in the sunshine. The Worm Moon embraces the awkward transition from death to life, from winter to spring, from dreaming to doing. Ugliness, therefore, must come before beauty.

The spring (or vernal) equinox marks the moment in the solar year when the day and night are about equal. Though we may not feel the warmth of the sun quite yet, we can certainly feel the light. We may have a bit more energy, a bit more focus for whatever work we are doing in the daytime. This was the original new year month for the Romans, who named this month after Mars, the god of war, as this was when the soldiers emerged from the cold winter to don their armor once again. The Sioux also counted the new year as the first new moon after the vernal equinox. Now, we can finally shift from the dark half of the year, which is all about dreaming, spiritual work, and connecting with intuition, to the bright half, which is all about extroversion, focus on the body, getting things done (though hopefully not through war), and enjoying the magic of the natural world.

The Wiccans celebrate the equinox as Ostara, a word that references an ancient Anglo-Saxon goddess of the spring. Her name, also sometimes written as Eostre, refers to the dawn and the coming of the light, which likely references the Greek goddess of the dawn, Eos. This was a day to plant seeds, feast, and honor the goddess' symbols of fertility, including hares, who generally mate during this season, and eggs, an obvious symbol of new life and new birth—symbols that you'll tend to see associated with modern Easter celebrations.

For the Anishinaabe and Ojibwe, this lunation has a sweeter name: the Sugar Moon. Despite the often still-cold temperatures, sugar maples take some mysterious cue from the light near the equinox and begin to flow. Maple syrup feels like a delicious and energy-rich gift emerging from the long, cold winter season. It takes work to extract maple syrup from maple sap, but it is a golden nectar, a delicious initiation into a new season, replacing the calories that were lost during January's hungry Wolf Moon.

Welcome to the life-giving, awkward, wriggly, ugly, beautiful Worm Moon.

NOWRUZ

In Iran and other parts of the world with Persian influence, Nowruz is celebrated on the spring equinox as the Persian New Year. This is an ancient holiday with roots in Zoroastrianism, a religion that predates both Christianity and Islam. Nowruz (or Norooz, or other spellings) means "a new day" and it celebrates renewal and rebirth. Nowruz has some similarities to the Lunar New Year celebrations: people deep clean their homes in preparation for the festival, which involves thirteen days of feasting, bonfires, and giving money to children for good luck and a fresh start. Families will gather symbols like apples for health, a lotus fruit representing love, and new grass for rebirth and place them somewhere visible to invite these things into their lives.

SEASONAL WELLNESS

- Get outside more. Look for those signs and signals of the earth coming back to life. You might even see some small shoots and buds starting to make themselves known. Let this encourage your spirit.

- Take some time to meditate on desire. What do you want right now? What sparks your passion?

- Slowly start incorporating more fresh fruits and vegetables into your diet as the world warms up, but take it easy. If it's still quite cold where you are, stick with warm, cooked foods for a little longer.

- Incorporate some maple syrup into a meal somewhere. As you do, take the time to consider this sweet tree nectar that flows only in the late winter and early spring.

- Close to the spring equinox, the energy is relatively balanced. You may find that more active movement is more available at this time, such as more vigorous yoga classes, dance, walking, running, or whatever movement feels best for you and your body.

- The spring equinox is a time for planting seeds, both literally and metaphorically. Work on your garden, if you have one, and start clarifying the intentions you've been gestating all winter and maybe putting some things into action. If you're more of a houseplant kind of person, go out and get a new one to tend.

JOURNAL PROMPTS

What seeds am I planting in my own life and body at the spring equinox? What is wriggling to the surface for me now like the worms in the March dirt?

AFFIRMATION

I allow light, hope, warmth, and possibility to return at their own pace.

THE ACE OF WANDS

In the tarot deck, wands represent fire, passion, energy, and spirit. The ace often shows up when a new passion arises or when some other new energy is trying to come through to invite change. The March lunation invites us to connect with our inner fire and take action on our desires. The ace is the most elemental card of the wands suit, the messiest, most unformed version of this energy. It's worms wriggling just under the dirt, the ground coming back to life after a long, dark freeze. It's pure energy, not quite formed yet, shaking things up and heralding change. It's messy, it's awkward, and it's good.

ACE OF WANDS

YOGA POSE

WARRIOR ONE

When the god Shiva lost his first wife, Sati, in a moment of injustice, he threw one of his dreadlocks on the ground in a fury of passion, and it transformed into Virabhadra, the fierce warrior. Virabhadra reached up through the ground, arising to fight against injustice. Warrior One, or Virabhadrasana I, represents this pushing up through the earth to cause change, much like the energy of the churning earth of the Worm Moon.

From standing, step your right foot back in a long walking stride. Allow your back foot to turn out at about a 45 degree angle with your heel on the floor. Your feet should be about hip-width apart.

Ground your back foot down as you square your hips and chest forward toward the short edge of your mat. Bend your front knee until it is over your ankle.

Reach your arms up to the sky with your palms together, as if you are driving up out of the earth to fight for justice.

Hold for five deep breaths, and then gently switch sides.

SEED RITUAL

The Worm Moon is a time to welcome back the light, to acknowledge what is wriggling just beneath the dirt, finally thawing after a long, dark, frozen season. Let's get our hands dirty with a seed ritual.

Please gather:

- A candle.

- Some dirt and seeds or a favorite plant, especially if one needs to be repotted. If the weather is good enough, you could do this ritual with the plants in your garden.

- Some clean, clear water, symbolizing Eostre's morning dew. This could be even more powerful if it is moon water (learn more about this in Making Moon Water in The Magic of Eclipses).

Take a moment to sit and get comfortable. Light your candle. Imagine a circle of protection around you filtering out any unhelpful energies and only allowing in the energies that are in alignment with your highest good. Then take a moment to acknowledge the land.

Place your hands gently on (or in) your dirt. Feel its potential, the possibilities it can nourish in its dark spaces. Consider your wishes, hopes, and dreams, whatever you have been gestating just beneath the surface. Imagining sending your wishes or intentions into the seeds. When you are ready, plant the seeds in the dirt if you are using them. Offer them some of the water and then drink the rest, solidifying your intention to turn toward growth, both within and without.

When this feels complete to you, thank the plant, the dirt, the seeds, the earth, the land, the air, the water, your circle, and anyone or anything else that needs thanks right now. Imagine your circle closed but never broken. Take good care of your growing seed or plant in the coming months.

THE MAGIC OF ECLIPSES

WHY DO ECLIPSES HAPPEN?

Moon drama happens because the earth rotates around the sun once a year, the earth spins around itself once a day, and the moon cycles around the earth every month. Twice a month, the moon aligns with the earth and the sun. But the moon's cycle is not a perfect circle, and its tilt means that alignment changes from time to time. Twice a year, the moon, sun, and earth align so perfectly that the conditions become possible for an eclipse—this is called an eclipse season. It lasts about 35 days, and the moon cycles through its phases every 29.5 days, which means there are always at least two eclipses during an eclipse season.

Due to a little bit of cosmic luck, the moon and the sun appear to be about the same size from our perspective on earth. The sun is a full 400 times as large as the moon—but it is also exactly 400 times farther away, so the relatively tiny moon can obscure the massive sun for us from time to time. While eclipse seasons are relatively common, experiencing an eclipse is less so, especially a total eclipse. That's because there is only a small area of the earth where the moon's shadow hits the earth perfectly, creating the conditions for a total solar or lunar eclipse. It only takes a few hours for this phenomenon to happen completely, so our perfect shadow may land in the ocean, for example, too far out for us to experience with our own eyes.

If you're lucky enough to experience a total solar eclipse, it is a powerful and beautiful experience. At any given place on earth, a total solar eclipse will only happen every 360 to 410 years.

A total lunar eclipse, on the other hand, happens a bit more frequently. When the moon is full but travels behind the earth, it is obscured by the earth's shadow. Compared to the moon, the earth is relatively large, so there is plenty of shadow for the moon to hide behind. Total lunar eclipses happen around every year and a half.

During a total lunar eclipse, the moon is completely in the earth's shadow. However, the light of the sun travels through the earth's atmosphere and hits the moon indirectly, creating a reddish glow, like a sunset, over the face of the moon. This has become known as a blood moon.

ENERGETICS OF ECLIPSES

Many of the ancients feared the Blood Moons. If you didn't understand why the moon would suddenly turn red from time to time, you might think it a terrifying omen. Solar eclipses were even scarier—the sunlight we rely on suddenly turning black in the middle of the day must have been quite a shock. Some witches caution that eclipses (especially solar eclipses) are not a time to do major spellwork, but rather a time for reflection and rest. Others wish to harness the powers of this special time and take the opportunity to supercharge their intentions.

Eclipses intensify the energy of the moon. The precise alignment of the three heavenly bodies means that the pull of gravity will be at its maximum. Solar eclipses will send you deep into your shadows, and lunar eclipses are powerful times to shed and let go. Eclipses also support transitions and change, so take this time to mindfully clear whatever might be in your way so you can move forward.

MAKING MOON WATER

A lunar eclipse is a perfect time to make moon water. You can do it during any full moon, but an eclipse will supercharge the water.

- Find a clean glass jar with a lid and fill it with clean water.

- Hold the water in your hands and send it your intentions or wishes.

- Place the water in the moonlight during the eclipse. Outside or on a windowsill is fine. You could also bring it with you for a moonlit picnic.

After the eclipse, you can drink the water for extra energy, offer it to a pet who may need some support or healing, bathe with it, or water your plants with it to give them a little boost.

HARNESSING SEASONAL LUNAR ECLIPSE ENERGY

WINTER SOLSTICE ECLIPSES: An eclipse season near the winter solstice is a powerful time to rest and reset. It's a forceful command for you to stop what you are doing, rest, and recover. You may naturally be feeling some exhaustion or burnout as the year comes to an end, so listen to the signals of your body and take that time out.

SPRING ECLIPSES: These are about movement, action, and starting or building something new. It is a generally optimistic season, a good time to put your plans and intentions into action. Clear out whatever limiting beliefs have been holding you back during this time—maybe even write them down and burn them under the light of the red blood moon. Stop stalling and start doing.

SUMMER SOLSTICE ECLIPSES: An eclipse near the summer solstice invites you to reflect on what has been cultivated by you at this point. Pause to enjoy the fruits of your labor and slow down on doing for a little while. Reflect on what's been working for you and resolve to let go of whatever has not. This is an excellent time to celebrate, gather with loved ones, feast, and maybe even howl at that red blood moon.

AUTUMN ECLIPSES: The autumn equinox is a season of death and endings, so an eclipse during this time may feel a little darker but also a little more magical. This is a powerful time to release, cleanse, and let go of whatever has been holding you back, and you may find there are big, intense movements to help you shift into a new phase of your life.

BIRTHDAY ECLIPSES: When an eclipse falls near your birthday, especially if on the actual day of your birthday, you must pay attention to your life path. Change is possible, if not inevitable, during this time. You may be shifting to a new career path, into or out of a relationship, or learning new things about yourself. This can be wonderful if you work with it mindfully.

SOMA: GOD OF THE MOON

In Hindu mythology, the god of the moon is named Soma (or sometimes Chandra). In addition to being the god of the moon, he is also personified as *soma*, a mysterious plant that provides immortality. The moon waxes and wanes, as the story goes, because the gods are sipping away at the moon's *soma*, taking a little bit of its light, and then allowing it to regenerate before they go back for more. Some say the ancient Tantrics would ritually consume a plant that had psychoactive properties that they referred to as *soma*. Among other things, these rituals had the effect of reminding the devotees that God is within everyone and everywhere, that there is no separation between the mundane and the divine.

Metaphorically, consuming the light of the moon intoxicates us. It can temporarily free us from the bonds of our everyday lives and remind us of our fundamentally divine nature. When we spend time in this state, the little things no longer feel important and we can get closer to what really matters to us in our lives. If you make moon water (see Making Moon Water above), you might consider this to be your *soma*, your magic nectar of the moon.

In a famous story from Hindu mythology, the angels and the demons cooperated for a time to churn the Ocean of Milk—also known as the Milky Way—to discover the nectar of immortality, here called *amrit*. When they finally found it, a demon named Rahu immediately took a sip. The Sun and the Moon noticed this and alerted the gods, who immediately sliced off his head. Having swallowed the *amrit*, however, Rahu stays alive as a head and a body separately. It is said that the eclipses happen because of Rahu's attempt at revenge: his head attempts to bite the Sun during solar eclipses while his body attacks the Moon during lunar eclipses.

APRIL

AWAKENING MOON

Names of the Moon

Neo-Pagan: Awakening Moon

Old Farmer's Almanac: Pink Moon

Chinese: Peony Moon

European: Egg Moon

Celtic: Growing Moon

English Medieval: Seed Moon

Wiccan: Seed Moon

Colonial American: Planter's Moon

Cherokee: Flower Moon

Algonquin: Breaking Ice Moon

Dakota Sioux: Moon When the Streams Are Again Navigable

Anishinaabe: Suckerfish Moon

Roman: Aperio, "to open"

STEP INTO A NEW SEASON

April was memorable when I lived in the wintry eastern Canadian city of Montreal. It would snow, classically, on the second weekend of the month, and then the following week it was summer. No in-between—suddenly every flower was blooming, spraying petals on the sidewalks, the hot sun cheerfully inviting the entire city out to drink and socialize on the patios. Any hint of a chill in the air was studiously ignored in tank tops, shorts, and sandals. It was such a relief after the brutally cold and windy winters there, I remember watching the rivulets of snow melting along the sides of the field at my school and thinking "I survived. My god, I survived the winter again."

The Old Farmer's Almanac popularized the name Pink Moon for this lunation, which apparently came from a North American indigenous tribe (or several) but it doesn't name specifically which one(s). This name refers not to the color of the moon, but to the blooming of pink moss phlox, a wildflower native to the eastern and central US that shows up like a bright pink carpet in the spring.

For the Algonquin, this is the Breaking Ice Moon, when the frozen stranglehold of winter finally breaks. The Dakota Sioux call this the Moon When the Streams Are Again Navigable, which feels so right to me. We can finally start moving again, as if the sap in our veins goes from frozen to flowing, our inner streams again becoming navigable. The birds, trees, and flowers that begin to open their faces to the sun are Awakening, as the Neo-Pagans have named this moon, and so are we. This awakening energy can be a little awkward, like the winter blinking its eyes awake to the spring after a long sleep. April showers bring May flowers, and the days can oscillate between cold and wet and warm and sunny.

The ancient Roman name for April comes from the word *aperio*, which means "to open": an aperture into the new season, a portal, the welcome moment when the flower buds open to the sun. Desire and sexual energy can wake up with the natural world, and some say this is the perfect season to conceive a baby—though that energy is well used for conceiving a project or idea as well.

Then it was spring; and in spring anything may happen. Absolutely anything.

~ E.E. CUMMINGS

As Christianity spread throughout the world, it often absorbed (or competed with) traditional rituals to allow people to convert without completely leaving behind the rituals that were most important to them. Easter, which is often celebrated in April, is always placed on the first Sunday after the first full moon after the equinox, so it relates to the Ostara rituals of the vernal equinox in March. It also lands around the same time as Jewish Passover, which remembers the liberation of the Jews from slavery in Egypt. Both holidays are oriented around the paschal full moon, the first full moon after the spring equinox, with the word *pascha* meaning "passover."

While Easter officially celebrates Jesus' resurrection three days after he died on the cross, we tend to symbolize this holiday with chocolate eggs and images of bunnies, both symbols of Ostara and the fertile goddesses of spring (Eos, in particular, was known for having quite the libido). There weren't any chocolate eggs or bunnies in Jesus' empty tomb that we know of, but, symbolically, the death and rebirth of God's son parallels the death and rebirth of the earth's sun, which comes back to "life" after the vernal equinox.

The Awakening Moon reflects the natural cycle when the sun finally reappears after seeming to "die" in the long, dark, cold nights near the winter solstice. Naked grey trees go green again, a spring coat of new leaves appearing on their branches. Perennials who were absolutely coated in frost and snow all winter cheerfully recover themselves, ready for another cycle of life and procreation. When we allow ourselves to be in tune with these natural rhythms, we are likely to find new hope in the fresh sunshine and flowers. May April's Awakening full moon gently rouse us from our winter slumber.

SEASONAL WELLNESS

- It's a good idea to get outside every month of the year, but while this might be a short walk in pale daylight in December, in April it's a leisurely stroll, soaking up the scents of the flowers that are now in bloom, and allowing the new spring sun to warm our skin.

- April showers bring May flowers, so take care to stay warm and dry on the colder, rainier days (but don't be afraid to get outside with a raincoat on).

- Receive color in the natural world. Take the time to pause and notice the colors of the flowers that are blooming in your region. Consider dressing to match, as a brighter spring wardrobe may help you keep your spirits up, especially if it's raining. Red or yellow rain boots, if you don't mind.

- You can begin to eat more fresh, in-season foods now as your system wakes up its digestive fire with the Awakening Moon. Slowly begin to incorporate more raw foods.

- Local honey is especially helpful as it may help ward off some of this season's allergies.

JOURNAL PROMPTS

What is awakening within me?
What energies am I ready to welcome into my body and into my life?

AFFIRMATION

I invite pleasure, movement, and breath into my body.

THE KNIGHT OF CUPS

The Knight of Cups rides in on his white horse, ready to sweep us off our feet, like a spring full moon on a warm April night. He is the romantic of the deck, the one bringing charm, beauty, romance, sexuality, and action. Cups represent the realm of emotion, relationships, and love in the tarot deck. Knights are well into their quests; they are seeking a prize, and they know something about how to get what they want, but they haven't quite achieved it yet. Knights have horses—they can take you somewhere, and fast. This is the energy of the Awakening Moon, which wants to whisk you away to a place of creativity, exploration, love, romance, and pleasure. As with all knights, however, don't gallop too fast into your big plans. Make sure you are learning your lessons as you go, lest you end up in the Underworld like Inanna (see Mythology later in this month). Take care of your heart, let it bloom and grow with the spring light, but don't forget to protect it at the same time.

KNIGHT OF CUPS

YOGA POSE

GODDESS WARRIOR

Goddess Warrior is a powerful, wide-open pose, reaching toward the sky, but grounded in the earth. It invites the powerful opening energies of the Awakening Moon.

Step your feet apart by about a leg's length with your left foot pointing toward the short edge of your mat and your right foot pointing toward the long edge (or slightly forward). Your front heel should be roughly in line with the arch of your back foot. Bend your left knee over your ankle, working your thigh toward parallel with the earth (and you may need to lengthen your stance to do this).

Open your arms out wide to the sides (which is Warrior Two), then reach your left arm up to the sky, allowing your right hand to rest on your back leg. Look up if your neck is comfortable with that. Hold for five breaths, then gently come out and repeat on the other side.

INTUITIVE MOVEMENT RITUAL

April is a time to wake up, to feel the water flowing through your body, to move, and to encourage the erotic energy that moves you toward creativity, pleasure, and, maybe, love. We need to include our bodies in this ritual and allow them to help us wake up and feel that inner ice breaking. All you need for this ritual is some space, some music you like, comfortable clothes, and some privacy.

Start in child's pose or laying on the ground. With your eyes closed, visualize your circle of protection around you filtering out any unhelpful energies and only allowing in the energies that are in alignment with your highest good. Take a moment to acknowledge the land you are on and your relationship with it. Depending on where this full moon lands, you may be in the wet, cold precipice of spring earlier in the month, or you may already feel the warmth of the sunshine returning. Check in with how the season feels in your body.

Keeping your eyes closed for as much of this as possible, simply begin to move. Move in any way that feels right for you, and feel free to dance if the music inspires that. You do not need to know what to "do;" simply follow your breath and the music and see what happens. Stretching, tapping, reaching, wiggling; it doesn't matter, and no one is watching. Take your time to slowly work your way up from the ground so that eventually you are standing. Keep moving just as long as you want to, allowing your body to call the shots. There is medicine in this movement, and you might be surprised to find that your body feels really good after this practice.

When you are ready, come to standing in stillness. With your eyes closed, simply receive this experience of awakening in your body. Notice how you feel now. You may also want to ask your body to communicate anything it wants to let you know. Thank your body, your circle, the land, the music, and whatever else you want to offer gratitude.

Eventually, open your eyes again and move on with the rest of your day. Your circle is closed, but never broken.

INANNA AND PERSEPHONE RETURN TO THE LIGHT

The ancient Mesopotamian goddess Inanna, the Queen of Heaven, was a goddess of love, fertility, and war. One day, Inanna decides to visit her sister, Ereshkigal, the Queen of the Dead, in the underworld, perhaps to challenge her sister's power. She encounters seven gates, and at each one, the gatekeeper requires her to remove some item of clothing or finery, her crown, her jewels, her dress, and so on, so that when she arrives at the heart of the land of death, she is completely naked, stripped of her icons of power. Having entered this realm of death, Ereshkigal decrees that Inanna must die, so she kills her and hangs her corpse from a hook on the wall. For three days, Inanna is gone, lost to the darkness of the underworld, just like Jesus and the sun during the winter solstice. While she is gone, the world above begins to die. The animals do not procreate, the bees do not pollinate the flowers, and the natural world grinds to a halt in the mourning of winter.

Inanna's followers are desperate for her return and the return of the living world above. They ask for help from her father, the god Enki, who sends two attendants to trick Ereshkigal into returning Inanna's corpse to them. The goddess is revived from death, but someone must take her place. An agreement is reached where her lover, Dumuzi, must spend half the year in the underworld, causing a winter of grief for Inanna, and his sister, Geshtinanna, spends the other half there, allowing Inanna to bring back spring and summer in her joy and love with Dumuzi.

There is an echo here of the Greek myth of Persephone, the daughter of Demeter, Goddess of Agriculture. Noticing Persephone's beauty, the god Hades, ruler of the underworld, abducts her to become his wife. While Persephone is lost in the underworld, her mother can think of nothing but finding her. She halts all her work, which means no grain grows, no edible plants are available, and the natural world begins to die, as it appears to in the winter.

When Demeter finally retrieves her daughter, the world celebrates, coming back to life. However, while she was in the underworld, Persephone ate the food of that place in the form of six pomegranate seeds (interestingly, pomegranates are another symbol of fertility, sexuality, and goddess energy). A deal is reached that Persephone lives in the underworld for six months of the year, causing her mother to mourn and withdraw each winter and return to life when her daughter comes back to her in spring and summer.

Inanna and Perspehone's stories reflect the underworld experience that many of us go through in the wintertime when the natural world appears to have died. But she also symbolizes an important psychological experience, which is ending up in a dark place, especially after we've made a mistake. Inanna is lucky enough to get a second chance at queenhood after her attempt to take something that wasn't hers to rule, and it is said that she became an even better queen after this ordeal, having come to understand her darker side. When we struggle in the darkness, as Jesus, Persephone, and Inanna have done, we may be reborn again, the same but different, having learned something we needed to know.

MAY

FLOWER MOON

Names of the Moon

Anishinaabe: Flower Moon

Algonquin: Flower Moon

Dakota Sioux: Moon of Flowers

Cherokee: Planting Moon

Neo-Pagan: Grass Moon

Celtic: Hawthorn Moon

English Medieval: Hare Moon

Wiccan: Hare Moon

Colonial American: Milk Moon

European: Milk Moon

Chinese: Dragon Moon

Roman: Maia, Goddess of the Earth and Plants

BLOSSOMS AND BLOOMS

May is a joy in pretty much every city I've lived in. In the colder climates, the snow has gone and the sun is warm but not yet humid and hot. Flowers are in full bloom everywhere, but on the Canadian West Coast in Vancouver, it is a wild festival of flora, with pink magnolia trees, bright multicolored rhododendron bushes, and the cherry blossoms—oh, the cherry blossoms! They don't always bloom in May, but when they do, it is an event. People hunt down the best parts of the city for cherry blossom watching and go and stand in a grove of trees, pink petals above them, scattered on the sidewalk below them, snowing on them gently. Some city sidewalks feel like wedding aisles at 10 a.m. on a Tuesday.

This moon is known as the Flower Moon in Anishinaabe and other North American indigenous traditions. The Roman name for May comes from Maia, an ancient earth goddess who presided over plants and flowers. For the Colonial Americans, it was the Milk Moon, a time when cattle are most productive. In the Celtic tradition, this was the Hawthorn Moon, the first full moon after the hawthorn tree bloomed. This tree was said to represent the Triple Goddess: blooming with white flowers in its form as the Maiden in the spring, ripe with red berries in its form as the Mother in summer, and then wrinkled and thorny in its Crone form in the fall and winter. When it bloomed in May, the hawthorn was a symbol of fertility and growth. It was sometimes called the May Tree.

The Celtic festival called Beltane, or May Day, falls on the first of the month. This was the traditional day for dancing around the maypole and decorating hawthorn trees with colorful ribbons. Young people would meet and court on May Day, enjoying the themes of playfulness, fertility, love, and romance as the flowers bloomed all around.

As we move deeper into the bright half of the year, our energies become more extroverted, more focused on the outside world and our bodies, rather than the deep inner soul reflections we tend toward in the darker half of the year. While in the fall and winter, we might be doing ancestor work, shadow work, and sitting with our intentions, the spring and summer are a good time for animal and plant magic and taking action on intentions.

You might notice that you are more suited to a certain part of the year: if you tend to be more introverted and intellectual, more drawn to the moon and imaginative/empathetic magic, you might actually feel somewhat more at home in the darker months (especially if you are allergic to all those blooming flowers). If you have more of a connection with animals, plants, and the extroverted energy of the sun, you might feel much more comfortable in the bright half of the year when you can spend most of your time outside with your hands in the dirt.

The May full moon is a time of joy, celebration, and tending to the seeds we've already planted. The fullness of this moon will pull on the tides of your body and your heart. Practice pleasure, joy, and hope. Your major task this month is to stop and smell the May flowers.

Very brief:
Gleam of blossoms in the treetops
On a moonlit night.

A lovely spring night
suddenly vanished while we
viewed cherry blossoms.

~ HAIKUS BY MATSUO BASHO

SEASONAL WELLNESS

- Go blossom-hunting. Get outside, even just within your neighborhood, and look for the flowers that are blooming now. Get your nose in there and smell them (but watch out for the bees).

- Tend the seeds you planted in the earlier parts of the year. This is a time for building and action, so keep the momentum up on whatever projects you have going.

- Celebrate Beltane. This might be as simple as lighting a fire to purify your intentions and make wishes.

- Attend to your fertility, whether literal or metaphorical. Gather the supports you need to feel strong and healthy, track your natural rhythms (especially if you menstruate), and focus on the projects that light your inner fire.

- Eat fresh, local fruits and vegetables now. Your body will start to be able to digest more cold, raw foods as the weather warms, so pay attention to your cravings and how they may be shifting.

JOURNAL PROMPTS

Where do I need the energy of blooming in my life right now? How can I encourage that flowering inside of me?

AFFIRMATION

I allow my body to teach me pleasure while I work toward my goals.

THE QUEEN OF PENTACLES

Pentacles (sometimes called coins or disks) is the suit in the tarot deck that is often associated with money, work, career, and practical aspects. But it is also connected to the element of earth, which speaks to the needs and wisdom of the physical body as well as our literal connection to the land. The Queen is someone who has mastered the challenges of her suit, in this case balancing practical needs, connection with nature, and connection with others. She is often shown sitting on a throne in a natural environment, surrounded by lush plants and flowers with a rabbit, symbolic of fertility and abundance, jumping at her feet. She holds a coin in her hands, cradling it lovingly. This symbol of fertility, grounding, love, and abundance is the epitome of the May Flower Moon. The Queen of Pentacles invites us fully into the bright half of the year and to enjoy sensual pleasures in balance with the meaningful work we must do to tend to our bodies and the material world.

QUEEN OF PENTACLES

YOGA POSE

GODDESS POSE

Goddess Pose, or Horse Stance, as it is sometimes known, is big, open, and symmetrical, representing the opening energies of the Flower Moon.

From standing, turn to the long edge of your mat, and open your feet apart by about a leg's length. Turn your toes out about 45 degrees away from each other.

Inhale, reaching your arms up to the sky.

Exhale, opening your arms into a cactus shape and bending your knees out to the sides.

Repeat this movement three times. Then hold Goddess Pose for three to five breaths with your knees and elbows bent. Take up space, breathing deeply, feeling the support of the earth beneath you. When this feels complete, you can simply return to standing and take a moment to feel the resonance of the pose.

FLOWER MAGIC RITUAL

Here is a simple ritual you can do to invite the energy of the May Flower Moon. All you need is to find a quiet spot outside next to a flower, whether a wildflower or one growing in a garden. Bring a journal and pen with you.

Sit quietly and imagine a circle of protection around you filtering out any unhelpful energies and only allowing in the energies that are in alignment with your highest good. Take a moment to acknowledge the land you are on. Feel the intimacy of your relationship to the land today, in this place.

Gaze at your flower. Notice the color, the texture, the smell, the plants around it, any bees or other insects trying to get close to it. Consider how it has opened itself for pollination, for fertilization, and how it is fully available to the bees who want its nectar for honey.

Draw this fertile, open, colorful, blooming energy into your own heart. Check in with how you are relating to this flower right now (or not). Respectfully ask the flower what it needs you to know to be open to creation and pleasure in your own life right now, and simply listen for any answer that arises. If it feels right, stay in conversation with this flower as long as you would like.

Write down any wisdom you may have gotten from the flower. Then write down what you would like to build or create in your life, where you would like the energy of this seasonal fertility to meet you in your own blooming.

When this feels complete to you, thank the flower for its wisdom and beauty. Thank the land and anything else that you would like to offer your gratitude toward. Place your hands on the ground, feeling your heartbeat moving in rhythm with the heartbeat of the earth.

Keep whatever you wrote down with you to refer to whenever you need to (or at your next full moon ritual).

SELENE

Selene is the ancient Greek goddess of the moon, known as Luna by the Romans. She is said to be a beautiful young woman with a crescent moon adorning her head, riding a chariot drawn by milk-white horses across the skies at night. She was born to two of the Titans, and her siblings are Eos, goddess of the dawn, and Helios, god of the sun. The ancient Greek poet Sappho wrote about her this way:

> "Rosy-fingered Selene after sunset, surpassing all the stars, and her light spreads alike over the salt sea and the flowery fields; the dew is shed in beauty, and roses bloom and tender chervil and flowery melilot."

Selene has the power of time, sleep, and the light that shines in the night, so she was also sometimes known as Phoebe, a goddess of the hunt. She later became equated with Artemis, the hunter, known as Diana in the Roman tradition.

Selene's love story is quite a strange one, both sweet and sad. It is said that Selene fell in love with Endymion, a mortal who was so beautiful he captured the moon goddess' attention while he was sleeping. Every night, she would visit him just to see the beauty of his face. In the Roman tragedy *Phaedra*, Seneca suggests that Selene's falling in love caused a lunar eclipse, which makes the full moon appear red for a few hours at night:

> "Or else, looking down on thee from the starry heavens, the orb that was born after the old Arcadians will lose control of her white-shining car. And lately she blushed fiery red, though no staining cloud obscured her bright face."

Selene would visit the sleeping Endymion every night, and eventually, the two bore 50 daughters called the Menai, a word that means "months." Each one represented the months of the four-year Olympiad, a common measure of time for the era.

Knowing that her lover's life would be cut short compared to hers, she petitioned the god Zeus to make Endymion immortal so he could be her lover forever. She knew, however, that immortality often comes with a price for human beings, so she adjusted her wish to allow him youth, beauty, and immortality in eternal sleep. Zeus granted her wish, and she was able to be with her sleeping lover forever. In some versions of the story, Endymion wakes up when Selene visits him at night and he falls in love with her as much as she does with him. In this version of the story, it is Endymion's wish to remain forever asleep so that he can dream of his love for all time. It's a happy ending for the lovers, sort of, but ironic that Selene's work as the moon is to constantly change and shift as she moves across the sky, while all she wants from her lover is stillness and sameness forever.

There aren't as many stories about female pursuit and desire in Greek mythology as there are about the gods, who often chase after unwilling human and divine women. Selene is filled with love, lust, and desire, and at least in some versions of the story, her love with Endymion is consensual. Desire is also present in her association with moonstone, which is written about in the *Dionysiaca* this way: "She wore also that stone which draws man to desire, which has the bright name of desire-struck Selene."

There is a parallel here to the Hindu and Tantric goddess Lalita, whose bow is loaded with arrows of desire. In Greek iconography, Selene is often shown standing above the sleeping Endymion. Similarly, Lalita is often shown standing above her supine lover Shiva, the Lord of Death (see the feature on Lalita: Queen of the Moon Goddesses).

As we cast our gaze upon the lovely moon, we find ourselves in the dark, at night, in the dreaming, spirit space where our joys can expand beyond the confines of waking life. This is a time to be with our wishes, dreams, and desires, and let the gods of the daytime worry about the rest.

JUNE

STRAWBERRY MOON

Names of the Moon

Anishinaabe: Strawberry Moon

Ojibwe: Strawberry Moon

Haida: Berries Ripen Moon

Dakota Sioux: Moon When June Berries Are Ripe

Colonial American: Rose Moon

Chinese: Lotus Moon

European: Flower Moon

Celtic: Moon of Horses

English Medieval: Dyan Moon

Wiccan: Dyad Moon

Neo-Pagan: Planting Moon

Cherokee: Green Corn Moon

Chocktaw: Windy Moon

Roman: Juno, Goddess of Marriage

MID-SUMMER STILLNESS

June is the month of the summer solstice (around June 21st), and the official beginning of summer. We've moved past the blooming of the Flower Moon, and are starting to see the first fruits of those flowers—namely, strawberries. In her book *Braiding Sweetgrass*, Robin Wall Kimmerer talks about the importance of strawberries in her tradition, the Potawatomi people. The Strawberry Moon was a time to look forward to, a time when the wild strawberries would appear like sweet gifts from the earth at her feet. She writes,

> "In our Creation stories the origin of strawberries is important. Skywoman's beautiful daughter, whom she carried in her womb from Skyworld, grew on the good green earth, loving and loved by all the other beings. But tragedy befell her when she died giving birth to her twins, Flint and Sapling. Heartbroken, Skywoman buried her beloved daughter in the earth. Her final gifts, our most revered plants, grew from her body. The strawberry arose from her heart. In Potawatomi, the strawberry is *ode min*, the heart berry."

The Strawberry Moon is a time of abundance. This is the peak of the solar year, when the sun itself is ripe and full, and the days are at their longest. In Neo-Pagan and Wiccan circles, the summer solstice is celebrated as Litha, when the masculine god of the sun is at his height and the goddess of the earth is nourished by his light, in turn bringing forth her gifts. This was said to be the time when the veils between the human and the faerie worlds would thin, inviting the potential for magic and blessings from the faerie realm. Like most of the Wiccan sabbats, Litha is a fire festival, a time to light a bonfire in honor of the sun and maybe even jump over it for good luck.

June was the traditional month for marriage. The name June comes from the Roman goddess Juno, protector of women, especially in marriage and childbirth. Ancient Celtic cultures also tended to celebrate marriages in June, shortly after the young people met and courted over Beltane in May.

While the light of the sun peaks in June, its heat tends to peak closer to July. In Vancouver, on the rainy West Coast of Canada, Junes are often not-so-affectionately called June-uary, as the late spring rains tend to make it feel much cooler and darker than we want this late into the year. The Strawberry Moon is a welcome shift from the wet nourishment of the spring to the warmth of the summer.

Summer solstice energy parallels that of the full moon itself: we are at a peak of brightness and the only place to go from here is back down to darkness. The word solstice breaks down to *sol*, which means sun and *stice*, which means stillness. The sun appears to pause in the sky at its peak, just as the full moon appears to rest, briefly, in its moment of total illumination. It is also a good month for us to pause, to look at what we have been building so far this year, and enjoy the fruits of those labors. All wild strawberries want in exchange for their gift is to be eaten, to be enjoyed, so that their seeds will have a chance to propagate for the next season. Similarly, this is a time to slow down and enjoy whatever abundance you have in your life right now. Eat the ripe fruits. Let the rest go.

In the Foothills

June, and everywhere I've been
All the sweetest petals have fallen
But here in the foothills of the Rockies
The peach trees just blossomed

I was long faced as I've ever been
thinking spring had gone gone gone.
Didn't enter my head for a second
that it had only moved up here.

~ JOHN MACKENZIE

SEASONAL WELLNESS

- Eat strawberries!

- Take a cue from many cultures that nap in the early afternoon when the sun is so high and so hot the only real option is to take a break. With longer daylight hours, you may need less night sleep: balance that out with a nap.

- Make pleasure a routine and a ritual: mindfully practice things you enjoy, such as good food, a beautiful walk outside, and the warmth of the sun on your face.

- Take some time out to acknowledge the work you've done on your goals this year. Celebrate the wins and let go of the losses.

- Invite and celebrate the energy of marriage. If you are married or in a partnership, have a special date to celebrate your love. If you are single, take yourself out on a date. If you're looking for love, light a candle with your wish for a partner. Then sign up for online dating, tell a friend you want to be set up, or ask your crush on a date.

- Celebrate Litha with fire: go to a bonfire at the beach with some friends or light a candle, welcoming the summer solstice.

JOURNAL PROMPTS

Write down what you're most proud of in your life since the last winter solstice as well as any lessons you learned or things you'd do differently next time.

AFFIRMATION

I celebrate myself and where I am in my life right now. I welcome light, positivity, and pleasure into my life.

THE SUN

The Sun tarot card is one of the most encouraging cards to receive. It is bright and positive, often showing sunflowers growing beneath a wide bright sun with a delighted, naked child sitting on top of a white horse. This card is the tarot version of the phrase "sunshine and flowers" and brings with it everything good. Its advice is to see the good in your life right now, to enjoy what's positive and present, and if things are feeling dark, to know that lighter times are coming. Of course, the dark side of the bright sun is that it can burn, too. The intensity of the light around the summer solstice can be a little too much, especially if you live in a northern place and want to sleep in past four in the morning when the birds start singing at sunrise. The Sun card can sometimes represent something that has been your Sun: someone or something that has been driving your life and taking all your attention, shining bright, possibly distracting you from your own inner spirit. Work with this energy in balance: honor pleasure, abundance, and light, but don't forget to attend to the shadowier places that are governed by the night and the moon.

THE SUN

YOGA POSE

BREATHE

Ujjayi is a breath practice that is often used in the context of a yoga practice as a way to connect the movements of a sequence together. The Sanskrit word *ujjayi* means "victorious," so it's a breath of power, sometimes called Breath of the Warrior. A gentler name is Ocean Breath, named as such because it usually comes with a soft sound reminiscent of ocean waves. The summer solstice is a moment of pause in the solar cycle. The energy peaks, but rather than push us forward, we are invited to stay here, to receive for a moment.

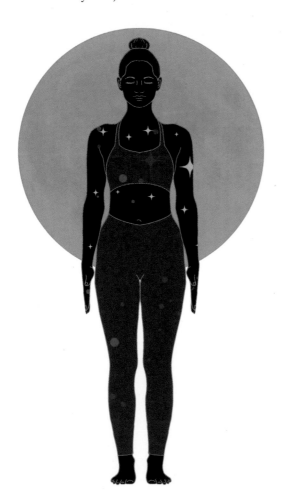

Stand comfortably in Tadasana, feet parallel, arms at your sides. Close your eyes and draw the breath along the back of your throat, creating a slight whispering sound. Feel the rising energy of each inhale, and the descending energy of each exhale. Stay like this for five (or more) deep breaths.

When you're ready, bring your breathing back to normal, which could include a sigh or just quiet breathing. Notice how you feel.

MINDFUL EATING RITUAL

For this lunation's ritual, we will eat a strawberry. Try to find a local one if you can. If you happen to be allergic to (or hate) strawberries, you could choose a different seasonal berry or anything that is safe for you that can symbolically stand in for a strawberry, like another fresh fruit, a sweet dried date, or heart-shaped cookie, for example. This is, essentially, a practice of mindful eating, which you can incorporate any and every time you eat.

Light a candle to signify the beginning of the ritual. Imagine a circle of protection around you filtering out any unhelpful energies and only allowing in the energies that are in alignment with your highest good. Take a moment to acknowledge the land that you are on and your relationship with it. Acknowledge the strawberry as a gift from this land.

Now observe your strawberry. Notice its color and its shape.

Contemplate its heart shape and its symbolism as a gift of love from the earth.

Smell it, with your eyes closed, and notice what that's like, if it brings up anything interesting for you, like memories or emotions.

Take a bite and feel it in your mouth, its texture and temperature. Taste it, seeing if the taste brings up any emotion or memory.

Swallow and observe how it feels to receive this gift into your body.

Repeat this process slowly and gently, staying present with the pure experience of eating the strawberry, how your body and the strawberry are in relationship with each other, and what changes as you consume the strawberry.

Mindfulness is a practice of noticing without judgment. This experience may not be 100 percent pleasurable, and it's okay if it's not. Simply notice what it's like and what happens for you in this experience. Is it challenging? Do you get distracted? Are there moments of joy? Do your best to practice this with curiosity rather than judgment or expectation.

When this is complete for you, thank the strawberry for its gifts. Blow out the candle, acknowledging the circle as closed but never broken. If you'd like, journal about the experience afterward.

LALITA: QUEEN OF THE MOON GODDESSES

In Shakta Tantra philosophy, the goddess is supreme. She is the energy that exists within everything, that animates life on earth and in the divine realm. All goddesses in this tradition are manifestations of the one Great Goddess, Shakti. One of these is Lalita, whose name means The Playful One. She represents the energy of desire, the drive that draws bees to flowers, the experience of beauty that can overwhelm us with awe, and the surge of desire that brings us toward our goals and toward each other.

Lalita is depicted as a sensuous young woman, overwhelmingly beautiful, dressed in red, which is the color of desire. She carries a golden lotus, which refers to enlightenment, and a cup of rubies filled with honey surrounded by bees. She carries a sugarcane bow with five flowery arrows, the arrows of desire. The Chief of Stars, or the Full Moon, rests in her crown.

Lalita is the queen of the Nityas, the Eternal Moon Phase Goddesses. Each one presides over a different night of the moon phases from new to full, and each reveals a different aspect of Lalita. She is present in all of them, though each one is separate within herself. Each of these goddesses speaks to an aspect of her wisdom and the philosophy of Shakta Tantra. The Nityas are as follows.

New Moon Night: Kameshvari Nitya, Goddess of Always Empowering Desire

Kameshvari carries the sugarcane bow with five flowery arrows representing the piercing experience of desire, of longing, and loneliness.

Second Night: Baghamalini Nitya, Goddess of Disruptive Desire

Baghamalini's name means "the flourishing garland" and she carries a red lotus and a night water lily. She represents the power of the lotus to grow from the dark earth through the muddy water to bloom at the surface.

Third Night: Klinna Nitya, Goddess of Embodiment

Klinna is adorned with unfinished gems and she is glistening with sweat. She carries a jeweled cup that catches the beads of sweat, turning them into nectar.

Fourth Night: Bherunda Nitya, Goddess of Vulnerability

Bherunda is unusual in the goddess pantheon in that she is naked. However, she carries more weapons than any of the others, including a shield that is also a song or a chant that provides her protection, revealing the hidden power in vulnerability.

Fifth Night: Vahnivasini Nitya, Goddess of Choice

Vahnivasini is adorned with gems like pearls and rubies that shine brightly on her crown. She is known as "Fire-Dweller" and "She Who Devours the Universe."

Sixth Night: Vajreshvari Nitya, Goddess of Intoxication

This goddess is red, adorned with red rubies, and her sari is red (red is the color of desire in this tradition). She is seated on a lotus flower perched on a golden throne in a golden boat that is floating on an ocean of blood. Her eyes "sway like red wine" and she is said to be intoxicated with her desire.

Seventh Night: Shivaduti Nitya, Goddess of Equality

This is usually the first quarter, the night when the moon appears halved in the sky. Shiva refers to the Great Goddess's consort, Shiva, the Lord of Death, which is not a bad thing in this tradition, but rather a necessary part of the cycle of everything. *Duti* is a Sanskrit word meaning "messenger."

Eighth Night: Tvarita Nitya, Goddess of Instinct

Tvarita's dress is made up of new leaves and her crystal crown is adorned with peacock feathers. She has a string of poisonous berries around her neck, and she is surrounded by wild animals roaring and howling with her.

Ninth Night: Kulasundari Nitya, Goddess of Learning

Kulasundari holds a book, which represents knowledge and learning from those that have come before us, and a golden pen, which represents our ability to change our story as we move forward into the future.

Tenth Night: Nitya Nitya, Goddess of the Death Light

The word *nitya* means "forever" or "eternal," so this goddess' name translates to Forever Forever. In addition to her gems, rubies, and flowery arrows, she carries a skull upturned like a cup she can drink from.

Eleventh Night: Nilapataka Nitya, Goddess of the Blue

While most of these goddesses are red or wearing red clothing (the color of desire), Nilapataka is all in blue. The word *nila* refers to a blue poison that arose when the angels and demons were churning the Milky Way to find the nectar of immortality, or *amrit*. For Nilapataka, the *nila* is the stuff that gets churned up when we do our deep healing or spiritual work. The *nila* is the *amrit*: the difficult stuff that arises when we do our deep work is exactly where we will find the sweetest nectar.

Twelfth Night: Vijaya Nitya, The Two-Faced Goddess

Vijaya, reclining on a sleeping lion, is said to be *saumya*, or sweet and easeful, when she is worshipped at night, and *ghori*, or terrifying, when worshiped during the day.

Thirteenth Night: Sarvamangala Nitya, Goddess of Freedom

Sarvamangala's name means "all auspicious." She holds a *matulunga*, a citrus fruit associated with healing in one hand, and a gesture of gift-giving in the other. The god of the sun, Surya, the god of fire, Agni, and the god of the moon, Soma, are with her.

Fourteenth Night: Jvalamalini Nitya, Goddess of Separation

Jvalamalini's name means "a garland of flames" and she carries many things in her twelve arms, including a shield and a tortoise, which represents the wisdom of withdrawing from the world from time to time.

Fifteenth Night: Citra Nitya, Goddess of Storytelling

The fifteenth night of the moon cycle is usually the full moon night. Citra is stationed in the ether, looking down at a *pura*, which is one of Lalita's cities of the mind. The other fourteen moon goddesses are there with her, and she watches from above. *Citra* is a word that means "painted" or "variegated" like the multicolored garment this goddess wears.

JULY

MEAD MOON

Names of the Moon

English Medieval: Mead Moon

Wiccan: Mead Moon

Dakota Sioux: Buck Moon

Colonial American: Hay Moon/Summer Moon

European: Hay Moon

Cherokee: Ripe Corn Moon

Anishinaabe: Raspberry Moon

Neo-Pagan: Rose Moon

Celtic: Moon of Claiming

Chocktaw: Crane Moon

Western Abenaki: Thunder Moon

Roman: Julius, Roman Emperor

SWEET HONEY SEASON

The Wiccan and English Medieval traditions refer to the full moon closest to the summer solstice as the Mead Moon. At this time of year, beehives are heavy with sweet honey that can be fermented into an alcoholic elixir called mead. Traditionally, June was the month to get married, so July would be the honey month, the honey moon, where newlyweds would be given enough mead to last a full month and be sent off to "get to know each other." If a son was born nine months later, the mead maker would be complimented on the quality of his product.

The Mead Moon is all about joy, celebration, pleasure, hope, and fertility. Like *soma*, the nectar of the moon that we discussed in March, mead is thought to be a nectar of the gods, a magical beverage that allows us to cast off the practical worries of our day-to-day lives and enjoy the present moment.

Mead has an ancient history, dating back at least to ancient Egypt, with evidence in civilizations the world over. It was especially important in Norse mythology, where mead was considered to be not only the nectar of the gods but also the drink of choice if you wanted intelligence and the ability to write good poetry.

While the summer solstice itself lands in June, the midsummer vibe really belongs to July. This is often a hot month with long days and plenty of opportunities to drink mead (or your beverage of choice) late into the evening with friends and neighbors. This is a time to enjoy the natural world, soak up the sun, eat the fresh fruits and vegetables of the land, and rest in sweetness. The summer solstice is a good time to pause on all our goals, and now is the time to observe. When you get to the peak of the mountain, you don't just head straight back down. You sit down, get out your snacks, and enjoy the view. July is the best time to take a holiday from work, if you can, to rest and enjoy the abundance of the natural world. The metaphor here is a perfectly ripe fruit that has grown from a tiny seed to become a juicy morsel. Eat it now: its very next phase is rot.

The full moon and the summer solstice share a similarly powerful energy, so this full moon may feel very intense—maybe even a little too intense. It can feel like there's a bit too much heat and brightness, the days are a little too long, and we may crave midday naps in dark, air-conditioned rooms and quiet time spent in the shade by the water, a cool drink at our side (and don't forget to hydrate, especially if mead is involved!).

Right now, the sun is at its peak. The sun is the purest form of yang energy in traditional Chinese medicine and ancient Buddhist thought: it's all about brightness, movement, intensity, heat, and doing rather than being. The moon is more related to the feminine realm, the dark, cool, quiet, yin aspect of everything. In July, we are at the height of Sun Season, the pinnacle of those yang energies. But just as in the yin/yang symbol, there is a dot of black at the place where the white is at its fullest and vice versa: the peak moment of yang energy will ultimately give way to yin. The Wiccans believe that the summer solstice is a season when the God of the Sun is in his primacy, and his power nourishes that of the Earth Goddess, bringing her into her fullness. These energies support and dance with each other, and we may paradoxically be feeling them both intensely at this time.

July's full moon is also sometimes called the Rose Moon. While the roses are certainly in bloom during this season, this month's moon tends to sit a little lower in the sky, which can give it a pinkish hue as it reflects through the earth's atmosphere, adding a rosy glow to our honeymoon month. Farmers in Europe and England also sometimes call this lunation the Hay Moon, as hay could be harvested in the early morning and late evening light at this time of year. July is a time to take advantage of the warmth, abundance, and long days: make hay while the sun shines.

SEASONAL WELLNESS

- Enjoy the fruits and vegetables that are in season right now. Your body will be primed to digest cold, raw foods at this time of year.

- Take a vacation, if you can, from whatever work you do. Relax and enjoy the long days and the sunshine. Put aside what you're doing for a little while and practice being.

- See this month as a yearly "honeymoon," a time to receive the fruits of your labor, including in your relationships. Step back from the grind and enjoy pleasurable experiences with the people you love.

- Incorporate water, where you can, both by drinking plenty of it and immersing your body in it. Spend time near the shore or set up the sprinkler for the kids. The yin coolness of the water will help to balance the heating yang energy of this time.

- This is an extroverted time of year, intended for spending time with others. Enjoy that, but make sure you balance it with quiet, calm times on your own so you can recharge.

- Continue to nap in the afternoons, at the hottest point of the day, if at all possible. You may find you can get up earlier and go to bed later, but you'll benefit from rest and darkness when the sun's heat is at its peak.

- As always, spend time outside whenever you can, enjoying the flowers that are blooming now. Depending on how hot it is where you are, you may want to do this in the early morning or late evening rather than in the full heat of midday.

JOURNAL PROMPTS

What is my relationship to pleasure? Do I seek it? Allow it? Reject it? Avoid or suppress it, for example by taking a picture of the moment rather than actually being in it?

AFFIRMATION

I receive sweetness and joy into my life.

THE EMPRESS

The Empress is the embodiment of the full sun and full moon of July. She is abundant, fertile, and feminine, a classic Earth Mother archetype. She is often shown on a cushioned throne out in nature, a crown of stars on her head, wearing a gown patterned with pomegranates, an ancient symbol of fertility. The Empress is about flow, emotion, sweetness, pleasure, enjoyment, abundance, and being rather than doing. Her advice is to soften into your experience, to notice the abundance that is already around you, and enjoy it fully, allowing yourself the pleasures of this time. Like a perfectly ripe peach, this time should be experienced and enjoyed right now, before the peach softens, bruises, and returns to the earth. Don't miss out on the gifts that are being offered to you in the present.

YOGA POSE

GATE POSE

Gate Pose is a simple side bend that also implies a gate, a portal through which we transition from one state to the next (and perhaps through which the faeries appear to greet us). We're through the portal of the summer solstice, and it's time to open to warmth and joy.

Start this pose on your hands and knees. Extend your right leg behind you and touch your toes to the floor. Turn the heel down, so that the toes face the long edge of your mat on the right (like a Warrior Two foot).

Gently swing your left foot behind you, keeping your knee down, so that the top of the foot or toes land off your mat to the left and you are supported by your left knee and left hand.

Reach your right arm up to the sky, turning your chest to the right side of the room. If you wish, take your arm alongside your ear to enhance the stretch on the right side of the body.

As you hold the pose, gently tuck your tailbone under, press your outer right foot to the earth, and turn your heart gently toward the sky. After three to five breaths, switch sides.

When this feels complete, you may like to come into Child's Pose to rest.

PLEASURE PRACTICE RITUAL

July is a wonderful time to ritualize pleasure practices. This is something you can do all month long, but perhaps especially on the day of the full Mead Moon.

Set your intention to hunt for moments of sweetness. Look for pleasurable experiences that you already have as a part of your daily routine: the morning coffee, the hot shower, the walk to work smelling the flowers along the way. Every time you notice a moment of pleasure, even if it's small, take a full breath and notice what happens in your body in a moment of pleasure. Take it in as fully as you can.

In addition, create pleasure for yourself wherever possible. Think about genuine pleasure, which means experiences where you are fully present in your body. Drinking too much, eating too much, or binging TV shows isn't pleasure, it's numbing, it's a way of getting out of your body rather than being in it. Genuine pleasure brings you closer to the experience of your body, which can be wonderful but also intense.

Be aware that sometimes genuine pleasure can bring with it a mix of emotions like sadness, anxiety, or guilt, alongside the enjoyment. Make space for those, but practice returning to the pleasurable sensations that are available right now. Let pleasure teach you something about your body and your inner world.

MEAD MYTHOLOGY

All over the world, honey wine is thought to have special, magical properties, conferring wisdom, health, love, fertility, long life, and more. In Norse mythology, mead was brewed from the blood of Kvasir, a man created from the spit of the gods and said to be the wisest person in the universe. He knew everything and contained all the wisdom of all the storytellers and poets within his body, and all he did all day was go around answering people's questions. Even he, however, had his weaknesses, and was tricked by the dwarves Fjalar and Galar, who killed him when he showed up to answer their questions.

The dwarves mixed his blood with honey, creating the Mead of Poetry, which could turn anyone into a scholar just by taking a sip. They hid it in three vats and told the gods Kvasir had simply choked on his own intelligence—a rather suspicious way to die.

Odin, the Allfather, father of the gods, found out about this. You can't get much past Odin—he is the wisest of the gods, and he went through a lot to get that way. In his quest for knowledge, he cut out one of his eyes in exchange for a drink of the god Mimir's well to give him enlightenment. He ritually sacrificed himself, then hung himself from Yggdrasil, the Tree of Life, for nine days and nine nights, receiving wisdom in the form of visions. His story is reminiscent of that of Inanna and Persephone, who descended to the underworld in a version of death, returning to life and the above world with new, darker knowledge. Odin also has a relationship with the Hanged Man tarot card, which depicts someone hanging peacefully upside down from a tree, indicating a period of forced pause in order to gain wisdom from a different perspective.

In any case, Odin found out about the dwarves' mead vats. His relentless search for knowledge would have required access to a drink that could help him know more, so he immediately went about stealing them. The dwarves met their end eventually, facing the consequences of their murderous ways, and the vats ended up in the care of a woman named Gunnlöd. Odin agreed to sleep with her for three nights in exchange for three sips of her mead. With each of the three sips, he swallowed the entire vat of mead, and then immediately turned into an eagle to bring the elixir home. The few drops that fell to the earth in his rush to abscond with a bellyful of mead are said to account for all the bad poets and storytellers in the world. The good ones are said to have been gifted Odin's mead directly.

AUGUST

DOG DAYS' MOON

Names of the Moon

Colonial American: Dog Days' Moon

Wiccan: Wyrt Moon

Dakota Sioux: Sturgeon Moon

Chinese: Hungry Ghost Moon

Anishinaabe: Blackberry Moon

Cherokee: Fruit Moon

European: Grain Moon

English Medieval: Corn Moon

Chinese: Harvest Moon

Chocktaw: Women's Moon

Celtic: Dispute Moon

Neo-Pagan: Lightning Moon

Roman: Augustus, Roman Emperor

SUMMER FADES AWAY

If I were to give August's lunation a name, I'd call it the Fading Moon. After the bright, magical rainbow of July, all the color seems to drain out of the world at once, turning a dry beige. The grass is brown, the flowers have wilted, and even the peaches, pears, and corn that are in full fruit at this time fit that sepia color palette. If it's been a particularly dry summer, you can sometimes already see some leaves littering the sidewalks from the trees that have given up early in the summer heat. We've moved past the celebratory mood of June and July, and while it's certainly still hot, bright, and unquestionably summer, we can begin to feel the waning—the fading—of the year.

The Colonial American name for August's lunation is the Dog Days' Moon. According to *The Farmer's Almanac*, the dog days represent the hottest and most intense days of summer, technically sitting (or sweating) between July 3rd and August 11th. These are long, lazy days, too hot for even the dogs to do anything but pant in the shade. Some people associate this time with madness—dogs and people are said to run wild with overheat, tending toward irritation and rashness. Think of Spike Lee's classic 1989 film *Do the Right Thing*, where an intensely hot summer day boils over with racial tension and ends with a riot, a fire, and tragedy. Despite all these associations, however, the real reason these are called the dog days is written in the stars.

In ancient Egypt, the Nile river would flood every summer, bringing with it fresh water for the soil. This was called the Inundation, and it was a welcome event for the parched climate. The Egyptians noticed that the waters would surge coincident with the dawn rising of Sirius, the brightest star in the sky. The timing of this event was so vital that the Egyptians began their new year on the first new moon after Sirius (known to them as Sothis) first appeared in the East.

Sirius is known as the Dog Star because it is part of the Canis Majoris or Greater Dog constellation. The star's official name is Alpha Canis Majoris. The Greeks thought Sirius itself contributed to the late summer heat, and its name comes from *seírios*, which means "scorching." The bright star does not affect the weather here on earth, of course, but it became known as an omen, for good or ill, of the dog days ahead.

August 1st also roughly marks the midpoint between the summer solstice and the autumn equinox, which is the beginning of the harvest season. Wiccans and Neo-Pagans celebrate this day as Lughnasadh, the first of three ancient Gaelic harvest celebrations (including Mabon and Samhain). This one honors the god Lugh, a warrior in Irish mythology who is also associated with grain and the sun. The Christians adapted this as Lammas, or Loaf Mass Day, when bread from the first of the harvested grain would be baked and brought to church. This festival would have felt a little like a county fair, which many of us still enjoy in August; this is often the best time to go eat ice cream and mini donuts and get on a rollercoaster ride at the local fair.

The Wiccans also refer to this month's moon as the Wyrt Moon, as it is an ideal time to work in the natural apothecary of "wyrts," which is an Old English word for healing plants and herbs. Part of celebrating the late summer harvest means acknowledging and appreciating the abundance of the earth, and our relationship with it, including the healing properties of its plants and flowers.

Depending on where the full moon lands this month, you may be deep in the dog days, the extreme heat of summer, needing to halt and rest, panting like a dog, trying to avoid madness. Later in the month, however, you might notice the first hints of fall, a lengthening of the shadows, and that sweet coolness that starts to return at night. It's the last sip of summer before the waning of the year begins in earnest.

Just as July's full Mead Moon has the energy of a ripe peach that must be enjoyed immediately, August's Dog Days' Moon is the peach that has gone a little soft, a little bruised, slightly fermented on the inside, already having begun its journey back to the earth. Rot may mean we can no longer enjoy the fruit in the same way, but it also indicates a shift to a new form of existence, a surrender to the inevitable cycling of everything from seed to fruit and back to earth again. The waning of the year (like the waning of the moon) is a time for processing and integrating, not necessarily for starting new things or setting new intentions. Enjoy your harvest.

SEASONAL WELLNESS

- If the Mead Moon is a time for a fun vacation, rest, pleasure, and enjoyment, the Dog Days' Moon is the nap you need when the adventure is over. If it's still very hot and dry, take it easy. Let go of any pressure you feel to be constantly outside just because it's summer (especially if you have air conditioning).

- Keep working with cooling foods like fresh, raw salads, local fruits, and vegetables.

- If you feel yourself becoming hot and irritated, cool your body down with a hydrating drink or dip in the water before you say anything you might regret!

- Corn is the harvest star of the season. Lughnasadh should be celebrated with a feast, ideally a picnic or barbecue outside with some cold beverages, freshly baked bread, and ripe corn on the cob.

- Head to the fair and have some fun with your family and friends (but don't forget your water and sunscreen).

JOURNAL PROMPTS

What is my relationship to control, surrender, and change? Are there parts of me that resist the turning of the wheel, that try to hold on to ripeness and avoid the rot? Could I imagine a form of surrender or letting go that would feel empowering for me?

AFFIRMATION

I surrender to all I cannot control.

THE WHEEL OF FORTUNE

The thing to know about the Wheel of Fortune is that it turns. When Fate appears in our lives, we have no choice but to surrender. Change is inevitable, as this moon teaches us, and it can be energizing, enlightening, or as oppressive as the dog days of summer. August's moon shows us how the colorful ripe fruits and flowers of summer that we've been waiting for all year inevitably turn to dry brown grass, golden corn, and yellow peaches. We get the first indications that the earth's abundance will be withdrawn again, so we must begin to harvest what we can and let go of what we can't. When the Wheel of Fortune appears, we are asked to remember what is and is not in our control. Surrendering can be empowering when we get really clear about where we have choices and where we simply do not. The Wheel of the Year is turning. Change is in the hot, dry air.

WHEEL OF FORTUNE

YOGA POSE

MELTING HEART POSE

Melting Heart pose, sometimes called Anahatasana or Puppy Dog Pose, is a lovely gesture of bowing to the earth, softening the heart, and gently opening the chest and shoulders. It's also like a mini version of Downward Dog, imitating a puppy wanting to play, an appropriate shape for the Dog Days' Moon.

Start on your hands and knees. Tuck your toes under and let your knees be a bit wider than hip-width apart.

Walk your hands forward and draw your bottom up and back, slightly behind your knees. Come up onto your fingertips so that your chest can hammock down toward your thighs, melting toward the earth. Most of your weight should be on your legs, your fingertips are simply providing some traction so that your chest can stretch and relax down toward the earth.

Your head could rest on the floor or you could keep it up. You can also be still here or gently rock your heart from side to side, softly stretching the chest and shoulders.

Stay for three to five breaths, then sit back into Child's Pose and rest.

WYRT MOON RITUAL

We will align with the energies of harvest, plant medicine, and gratitude with a Wyrt Moon spell jar (similar to the Spell Jar Ritual in January). The Wyrt Moon is all about harvesting plants that have medicinal properties, and there are many in season around August.

Gather your spell jar materials, including a jar with a lid and some salt. Then go out and find some wyrts to add to your jar depending on what you would like to focus on this full moon. Roses have a cooling, soothing quality and are excellent for supporting grief. Lavender is calming, cooling, and purifying; its name derives from the Latin *lavare,* which means to wash. Yarrow and meadowsweet are both anti-inflammatory, which can help calm wounds as well as anger. Dandelions are excellent for detoxification.

Feel free to explore your garden or the weeds and wildflowers growing in your area (working with respect, of course, and with an awareness of safety). Gather the plants that speak to you in some way that can help you create your spell jar.

Once you have your ingredients, light your candle and close your eyes. Take a few deep breaths and imagine a circle of protection around you, filtering out any unhelpful energies and only allowing in the energies that are in alignment with your highest good. Acknowledge the land you are on and thank it for its abundance and its medicine. Offer gratitude wherever else feels right.

Then focus on your intention for this spell jar. Place some salt in the jar first, as it represents cleansing and protection. Then carefully place your wyrts into the jar, considering their meaning to you for this spell.

When this feels complete, seal the jar with a lid. You may like to seal it again with some wax from your candle.

Offer thanks again and then close your circle. Place the jar on your altar, if you have one, or wherever would be most helpful to remind you of your intentions.

HUNGRY GHOST MOON

In many countries in East Asia, the full moon of the seventh lunar month is known as the Hungry Ghost Moon. According to Taoism, Buddhism, and possibly some folklore even predating those religions, this entire lunation is known as Ghost Month, a time when the veils between the worlds thin and the ghosts of our ancestors pay us a visit. By the fourteenth day, the full moon, the ghosts are said to be very hungry from their wandering and demand to be fed.

Much like the Mexican Dia De Los Muertos, the Christian All Souls Day, and Halloween, this is a time to honor our ancestors and the fearsome power of death. Hungry ghosts are assumed to be cranky, and the living go to great lengths to appease them. On the first day of the month, little paper symbols of things like money, cars, and TVs are burned as gifts to the dead. Pictures and mementos of the ancestors are brought forward to be remembered. On the day of the full moon, food is prepared three times as gifts for the ghosts. Some people avoid wearing red, as it's thought to attract the ghosts and put you at risk of getting possessed.

In one origin story, a Chinese monk named Mulian prayed to the Buddha to help his mother who had passed over. She was hungry, but ghosts can't swallow. The Buddha tells Mulian to feed his fellow monks instead and provide them with new robes. In a gesture of gratitude for these gifts, the monks pray for Mulian's mother, and she is reborn as a human, able to eat once again.

The metaphor of a hungry ghost is about a craving that cannot be satisfied. There is danger when we want something that is not meant for us—ghosts are not meant to eat. Mulian is advised to focus on the living human beings right in front of him, to feed those that can eat.

When our cravings take over our wisdom and we find we cannot get enough, cannot fill our bellies, it might be time to look at where we are placing our attention. Are we focusing our desires toward something possible and accessible, something that could satisfy a deep need in us? Or are we chasing the food of ghosts, that which we can never really swallow?

There's something about this season that feels a little bit magical. For the witches and pagans, it's a time for encountering the faeries and the spirits of the natural world, while for the Taoists and Buddhists, it's an inauspicious opening of the gates of the underworld, setting free the hungry ghosts. Whether you consider this time full of blessings, curses, or both, it's a good idea to honor the energies you don't completely understand, whether that's ancestors, faeries, God, or whatever else resonates for you. And don't forget to feed yourself.

There was no air; only the dead, still night fired by the dog days of August. Not a breath. I had to suck in the same air I exhaled, cupping it in my hands before it escaped I felt it, in and out, less each time...until it was so thin it slipped through my fingers forever I mean, forever

~ JUAN RULFO

SEPTEMBER

HARVEST MOON

Names of the Moon

Colonial American: Harvest Moon

Neo-Pagan: Harvest Moon

Dakota Sioux: Corn Moon

Anshinaabe: Corn Moon

English Medieval: Barley Moon

Wiccan: Barley Moon

European: Grain Moon/Fruit Moon

Cherokee: Nut Moon

Celtic: Singing Moon

Chinese: Chrysanthemum Moon

Roman: Seventh Month (from March)

THE SEASON OF BALANCE

The Harvest Moon is one of two moons during the year that have a relationship with the autumn equinox rather than the month itself. The full moon that falls closest to the equinox (around September 21st) is always known as the Harvest Moon, so it can land in September or October. If this full moon falls in October, September's moon can be known as something else, like the Corn Moon or Nut Moon. The full moon that follows the Harvest Moon is always known as the Hunter's Moon, so that may fall in October or November.

The full moon nearest to the equinox tends to rise around sunset for a few nights in a row, which was a boon to farmers wanting to harvest the season's crops a little bit longer into the evening.

The Harvest Moon is probably the most known full moon name of the year, likely thanks to Neil Young and his song of the same name, a sweet tribute to long-time love and romance. If you want to impress a date with the magical powers of moon gazing, take them out around sunset in September. The evenings are still warm and light enough to be out, and a full moon close to the horizon will tend to look larger in comparison with the skyline (even though this is only an illusion). When it's low in the sky, we are also looking at it through a bit more of the earth's atmosphere than when it's higher up, so it's likelier that this season's moon will take on a bit of a golden or orange hue, altogether making the Harvest Moon a particularly beautiful sight—one that might be given to poetry, moonlit dancing, or maybe even a first kiss.

Equinox is a word that means "equal night," and represents the moment when the daylight and nighttime are about matched. Many of us are ready for the return of sweater weather after the long hot days of summer, and our perspective tends to shift with the light as we begin to move toward the darker half of the year. As we move into September, we shift toward what I like to call Moon Season, where we start to work more with the cool, reflective, introverted, quiet energy of the moon. Many of us have a muscle memory of September as back-to-school season, and even if we haven't been to school in decades, we still often get that feeling that vacation is over and it's time to start focusing on our more intellectual projects, going inside and getting things done before the cold stillness of winter really hits. The autumn equinox can feel like an energetic new year.

And it is a new year, at least in the Jewish tradition. Rosh Hashanah, which almost always falls in September, marks the Jewish New Year. It precedes ten days of reflection and prayer called the Ten Days of Awe, in which it is said that God judges the living. This culminates in Yom Kippur, the Day of Atonement, where people take stock of their wrongs and work on doing better in the coming year. Among other traditions, celebrants eat apples dipped in honey, symbolizing a sweet year ahead.

The Celtic name for this month's lunation was the Singing Moon. Perhaps this refers to the birds who can sing again as the oppressive heat lifts or the wind that sings in the trees as it picks up in preparation for the fall. But it may also mean literal singing—the sweet sound of voices celebrating Mabon, the middle harvest festival that is held on the autumn equinox between Lughnasadh in August and Samhain in October. Mabon is a time to take stock of the harvest as it is, eat cakes, pick apples, and drink ale or apple cider while feasting with friends. It would likely have looked a lot like Western Thanksgiving.

The autumn equinox represents the very beginning of the darker season. For those of us that like to play in the dark with magic, meditation, and imagination, it is a joyful new year indeed. But it is also the waning time for the sun, and from here on out, every night will be longer than the day until the winter solstice in December. As things cool off and we return to work (or school), we may find our energy picking up again. This energy is best used for processing, integrating, and completing our projects before we put them away for winter. The season of deep rest and inner work is coming, so it's time to finish up our internal and external harvest on this Harvest Moon.

SEASONAL WELLNESS

- Harvest, of course: look at what you have been building. Give thanks for what's working and re-evaluate what isn't.

- Focus on processing, integrating, and finishing up the work you've been doing this year in preparation for the darker, colder season.

- The Harvest Moon is a classic time for romance and poetry. Spend time with your lover, write poetry or songs about your crushes, or light a candle and pray for romance on this full moon.

- The equinox is a time of balance between dark and light. Look at the major areas of your life that feel relevant now: for example, physical health, financial wellness, career, relationships, and creativity. Which of these areas is taking up too much of your energy? Which ones need more of your attention to help you find balance?

- Enjoy the local in-season fruits and vegetables. As the weather turns colder, you may start to want more warm, cooked foods and spices. Cinnamon, ginger, and pumpkin are all warming flavors to help your body transition to the colder season.

JOURNAL PROMPTS

Where do I need more balance in my life? What would be needed to invite more balance and equality?

AFFIRMATION

I seek balance in all things, in part through allowing movement and change.

THE LOVERS

The Lovers tarot card is all about harmony, balance, and perfection, very much the mood of the romantic Harvest Moon. The image often shows a naked man and woman, likely Adam and Eve in the Garden of Eden, an angel above them, blessing their union. This is a moment of ideal balance and equality between two souls, as perfectly equal as the day and the night near the equinox. The Lovers card depicts a soul marriage, two beings becoming one under the eye of a loving God. True balance, of course, wobbles. It is never static. Eve made a choice: she lost the garden but gained knowledge and free will. Perfection is nice, but has its limitations. Let's enjoy this perfect moment as fully as we can, precisely because we know it can't last.

THE LOVERS

YOGA POSE

SEATED TWIST

As we move through the autumn equinox, we consider themes of balance and equality. This simple twist allows us to balance the right and left halves of our bodies, soothing our lower backs, stimulating our digestion, and calming our nervous systems as we move toward the darker half of the year.

Sit on a yoga bolster, pillow, or cushion near the top of your mat. Have your feet about the mat's width apart. Allow your knees to fall to the right and follow them so that your chest and head are all moving to the right. Your right arm will come to the floor behind you, and your left arm can hold your left thigh.

Allow your left hip to lift from the ground so your whole body is in a spiraling twist.

If you like, add a neck stretch: gently hold your left knee with your left hand and draw your shoulders down your back. Gently release your right ear down to your right shoulder for a lovely neck stretch. Hold for three to five breaths, then gently bring your head back to neutral and switch sides.

When this is complete for you, return to center and gently roll your shoulders a few times. Look all the way to the right and the left and then rest your head in the center and take a few deep breaths.

BREATH PRACTICE RITUAL

The Harvest Moon is a good time to be working with themes of balance, equality, and partnership. This simple ritual can be done with a willing partner, or you could do it on your own with the earth itself.

Light a candle to signify the beginning of the ritual. Imagine your circle of protection around you filtering out any unhelpful energies and only allowing in the energies that are in alignment with your highest good, and acknowledge the land you are on and your relationship with it right now.

If you are doing this ritual with a lover or friend, sit back-to-back so you can feel each other's breath. Without speaking, breathe deeply together and line up your breath so that you are inhaling as your partner is exhaling and vice versa. Breathe together for about five minutes, and then when you are finished, tell your partner how it felt for you, and listen to them speak about how it felt for them.

If you are on your own, lie down on the earth. Breathe deeply, listening for the earth's breath, imagining that you could line up your inhales and exhales with the breath of the earth. Do this for about five minutes, then return to a natural breath and simply notice how you feel.

But there's a full moon risin'
Let's go dancin' in the light
We know where the music's playin'
Let's go out and feel the night

Because I'm still in love with you
I want to see you dance again
Because I'm still in love with you
On this harvest moon

~ NEIL YOUNG

CHANG'E AND THE MID-AUTUMN FESTIVAL

On the fifteenth day (the full moon) of the eighth month in China and other countries in East and Southeast Asia, it's time to celebrate the Mid-Autumn Festival. It's a three-day harvest celebration, usually landing in September or October, and one of the biggest holidays of the year. It's time to feast with friends and family and to remember the myth of the Moon Goddess, Chang'e.

Once upon a time, the earth was scorching with ten hot suns in the sky. The skilled archer Hou Yi shot down nine of the suns, allowing just one to remain, making the earth favorable for agriculture. The goddess Xiwangmu, the wife of the Jade Emperor, a goddess of life and death who presides over the Peaches of Immortality, noticed this and gifted Hou Yi with the nectar of immortality.

She only gifted him enough, however, for one person, and Hou Yi didn't want to become immortal if he couldn't do so with his wife Chang'e at his side. Chang'e was a beautiful young woman with milky white skin, cherry blossom lips, and hair as dark as night. Hou Yi hid the elixir away, but while he was out hunting, his apprentice Fengmeng attempted to steal it, forcing Chang'e to drink it herself. She began to float up toward the sky and decided to stop at the moon, not wanting to be any further away from her beloved husband. She stayed there forever, becoming known as the immortal Goddess of the Moon.

When Hou Yi discovered what had happened, he was heartbroken. Every night, he displayed Chang'e's favorite fruits and desserts, trying to make her feel less alone. He did this every night until the day of his death.

Every year, people celebrate Chang'e's story by feasting on her favorite foods, especially mooncakes, which are circular pastries filled with delicacies like lotus seed paste, egg custard, and red bean paste. This treat is so popular that the holiday is sometimes called the Mooncake Festival. Apples, pears, and pomelos are often shared or placed on an altar as an offering to the Moon Goddess. Sometimes children put on the pomelo rinds as hats to gain Chang'e's favor as she was said to particularly love this fruit. Lanterns are lit and families gather to spend time together, eat, and gaze at the beautiful full moon, said to be the biggest and the brightest of the year.

MENSTRUATION AND THE MOON

Menstruation and the moon have always had a relationship. A full lunation from new moon to new moon lasts about 29.5 days, which is pretty close to an average menstrual cycle. The word "menstruation" is related to the Latin word for month, *mensis*, which in turn comes from the Greek word *mene* for "moon."

We know the moon has an impact on the tides, and as beings made mostly of water, it makes sense that the moon might pull on the tides of our blood, as well. Scientifically, studies are mixed: some researchers in the 1980s found that a good chunk of people tended to menstruate with the new moon (around 28 percent), while later studies found no correlation between lunations and menstruations. Still others suggest that we likely used to line up with the moons, but that those cycles have been interrupted by modern light pollution and hormonal birth control. Whether or not it's scientifically proven, however, many of us feel that the moon impacts our cycles. Not only that, but where our cycles land with the moon may say something about what's happening spiritually or energetically for us at the time. If you menstruate, where is the moon when your cycle usually begins?

WHITE MOON CYCLE

Menstruating on the new moon (that is, your period begins within about three days of the new moon night) is known as the White Moon cycle. When you are on this cycle, you are most in alignment with the fertile powers of the moon herself, building with the waxing moon, ovulating with the full moon, and slowing down during the waning moon. This is the cycle that is most related to conceiving a child, caring for others, and/or birthing creative projects.

PINK MOON CYCLE

Menstruating during the waxing moon indicates a time of transition. You are shifting from a darker period in your life to a lighter, more expansive one, where you are putting your reflective work into action in a new role or in a new way. You may be shifting out of a time of deep self-work into a phase that is more focused on the outward, material world. This is a good time to shed any old beliefs that hold you back from going toward what you really want.

RED MOON CYCLE

This pattern of menstruation is to bleed during the full moon. This is the witches' rhythm: your intuition is likely to be deep and acute, and you may find you have a little more access to the spiritual side of things, including magic, ancestor work, and healing practices, both for yourself and for others.

PURPLE MOON CYCLE

If your menses lands during the waning moon,
you are also transitioning, but it is likely
that you are moving toward shadow work.
That could mean working on your inner self
through something like counseling or perhaps
moving toward a more magical time in your
life. Sometimes this happens because there is
some trauma or grief that needs to be processed
before you can move into a different phase
in your life. Taking the time to do your inner
work will help you work through this transition
and will likely also bring you closer to your
inner power.

OCTOBER

HUNTER'S MOON

———

Names of the Moon

Colonial American: Hunter's Moon
European: Hunter's Moon
Cherokee: Harvest Moon
Celtic: Harvest Moon
Neo-Pagan: Blood Moon
Wiccan: Blood Moon
English Medieval: Blood Moon
Anishinaabe: Falling Leaves Moon
Chinese: Kindly Moon
Dakota Sioux: Moon When Quilling and Beading is Done
Roman: Eighth Month (from March)

DEATH AND THE DAYS AHEAD

Like the Harvest Moon, the Hunter's Moon is named according to the autumn equinox rather than the month itself. While the Harvest Moon is always the full moon closest to the equinox, the Hunter's Moon always follows that, so it can land in October or November. This full moon also tends to rise around sunset for several days in a row, providing more light for the hunters preparing for winter.

The English Medieval, Neo-Pagan, and Wiccan name for October's full moon is the Blood Moon. Full moons that rise near the horizon can look a little reddish or orange, but it's likely this refers to the late harvest slaughter that was necessary for survival in the cold months to come.

It's a spooky name appropriate to the month that hosts Halloween. Known as Samhain in ancient Celtic tradition (pronounced Sah-wen), October 31st is a cross-quarter day, representing the midpoint between the autumn equinox and the winter solstice (though the actual astronomical midpoint might differ slightly). This is the last of the three ancient Celtic harvest festivals after Lughnasadh and Mabon, and it is the time to collect up the last of the season's gifts and prepare for the winter.

While Lughnasadh and Mabon focus on grain, corn, and other harvested plants, Samhain is about the harvest of the animals—the death harvest. Samhain was the traditional day to perform the slaughter. It is also said to be a time when the veils between the worlds thin, when ghosts and ancestors can visit the living.

The theme of death around this time is shared in many cultures. November 1st and 2nd are celebrated as Dia De Los Muertos, or the Day of the Dead, in Mexico. This is a time of reunion between the living and the dead, a celebration that includes feasting, costumes, and parades. Food is left out for the ancestors, much as it is in China during the Hungry Ghost Moon. The Christian tradition celebrates their version of these days as All Saints and All Souls Day. Death is in the air as we shift into the darker, colder part of the Wheel of the Year.

On the Canadian West Coast, the wind and rains have often returned by October, stripping the trees of their leaves. But some years the rains wait, leaving the trees thick with deep warm reds, raincoat yellows, and pumpkin orange. These are the colors I loved in the fall growing up in more eastern parts of the country, watching great swaths of trees seeming to synchronize with each other when some deep signal of light or cold told them all at once to change colors. It is a theatrical performance of death and dying, an offering of beauty that heralds a cyclic loss.

Samhain is the most important festival in the Wiccan Wheel of the Year, not only because it is a time for magic, but because it is also New Year's Eve. The flowers and fruits that we are gifted with in April and May are not the beginning, but rather the result of many months of work spent underground. This dark time isn't a bad thing, it should be honored and celebrated.

Halloween is a big deal in the US, Canada, Australia, and many other parts of the world. It's a strange day of play around the concept of death. We dress our children up as ghosts and monsters and send them off to collect candy from their neighbors, but we don't often talk openly with them about what it all means. We ignore the lessons from death on display all year as the trees and flowers wilt, appearing to die, only to be reborn again in the spring. Death is an important part of a cycle, and when we welcome that rather than avoiding it, we can embrace life all the more fully.

SEASONAL WELLNESS

- Embrace the season of death by remembering ancestors, lost loved ones, or even selves that you once were that you are grieving now.

- Explore your own connection to internal magic through practices like meditation, tarot, prayer, casting spells, and lighting candles.

- Spend time outside, as the weather allows, and enjoy the seasonal changes where you live. Go leaf hunting, just as you would go blossom hunting in the spring. The natural world, even in an urban environment, may look vastly different from one week to the next; watch for the synchronizing cycles.

- Drink warm teas and eat warm, cooked foods, especially nourishing root vegetables like squashes.

- The pumpkin spice flavor palette is perfect for fall. Ginger, cinnamon, nutmeg, and cloves are all warming spices that can help keep us balanced as we shift to a colder season.

- Cover the back of your neck with a scarf, especially if it's windy. Keep your feet warm with good socks and place a heating pad or water bottle on your back, around your kidneys or adrenal glands, to keep your energy warm and safe as the days cool.

- Remember that as the light wanes, we need more sleep and rest. Allow yourself to sleep more when you want to and when it's possible for you.

JOURNAL PROMPTS

What would you say to an older, near-death version of yourself? What would this older self say to your present-day self?

AFFIRMATION

I embrace the wisdom of death and endings and allow them to teach me about life and new beginnings.

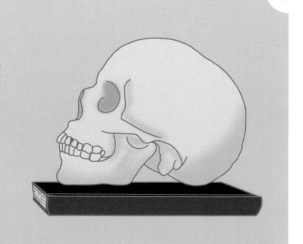

DEATH

The Death tarot card isn't necessarily about literal, physical death, but rather speaks to the end of something. It can be the end of a relationship, the end of a certain sense of self, the end of a chapter of one's life, and so on. In the traditional Rider–Waite–Smith version of the card, Death appears as the Grim Reaper, a skeletal figure on the back of a white horse, people of all walks of life powerlessly kneeling before him as the sun rises in the east. This ghastly figure arrives when your time has come, not to cut your life short, but to ease your passing to the other side. The position of the sun in the east of the card indicates that this ending will come with a new beginning. It's time to let something go, to thank and appreciate the death process for its necessary place in the cycle of life. Death is a difficult process, but it brings gifts. The gifts are sometimes hard to understand at first, but if we can stay open to them, they can bring a vibrancy to life that wasn't possible before.

DEATH

YOGA POSE

PIGEON

October's full moon is a good time to go deep, and Pigeon is the pose for that. It is a hip opener that gets into the part of our bodies that can sometimes carry old memories and traumas within it—our own personal ghosts. Spending time in Pigeon can bring these things to the surface to be released. Don't be afraid to breathe deeply in this pose, even making sounds as you exhale, to help let go of any energies that have been trapped in your hips. Ideally, do this pose with a bolster or long pillow and two yoga bricks.

Sit near the top of your mat on a bolster or cushion if you have one. Lean to the right and swing your left leg behind you. Do your best to straighten your back leg and adjust the angle of your front leg so there is no pain in your knee and your hips are supported on a prop.

Gently fold down over your right leg. Use your hands, elbows, or props to support your upper body. Stay for five to eight breaths. This may be uncomfortable but there should be no pain.

When you're ready, lean onto your right hip and return to seated, then wash your bent knees from side to side like windshield wipers. Repeat on the other side.

ANCESTOR RITUAL

Everyone has ancestors. Even if we were adopted and have no idea who our blood relations are, our ancestors are a part of us spiritually, energetically, and physically. A 2013 study in the journal Nature Neuroscience showed that a mouse whose grandfather was taught to fear the smell of cherry blossoms feared them too, even if he'd never encountered them in his life. Our ancestors are a part of us, even if we have no idea who they are.

Begin by lighting a candle. Cast a circle of protection around yourself in your imagination with salt, stones, or chalk (feel free to do this literally if you want to). Clarify that this circle of protection invites only loving, healing energy, and keeps out any energies that are not in alignment with your highest good. Acknowledge and honor the land you are on.

Take a few moments to calm your mind, perhaps by focusing on your breath. Then set your intention to communicate with one of your ancestors. Invite someone who wants the best for you and who is healed in their own journey. Request someone who can and will help you on your journey in life.

Wait patiently until you see someone joining you in your mind. Notice whatever you can about the person who comes to visit you. Are they male? Female? What are they wearing? Do they look familiar? How do you feel about them? Engage them in conversation. It's often easier to start with yes or no questions and make sure you are listening. Keep in mind that you are allowed to have boundaries with your ancestors. You do not have to do everything they say, and you can tell them to leave your circle if you feel uncomfortable.

When this communion feels complete, thank your ancestor for visiting you. Thank the land, the circle, and anything else that it feels right to honor. Gently return to your body in the present moment and remember your circle of protection. Imagine a shower of golden or white light cascading over your body and over your space, cleansing and clearing anything that should not come with you into the rest of your day. Blow out your candle to complete the ritual.

NOVEMBER

FROST MOON

Names of the Moon

Cree: Frost Moon

Anishinaabe: Freezing Moon

English Medieval: Snow Moon

Wiccan: Snow Moon

Celtic: Dark Moon

Chinese: White Moon

Colonial American: Beaver Moon

European: Hunter's Moon

Neo-Pagan: Tree Moon

Cherokee: Trading Moon

Chocktaw: Sassafras Moon

Dakota Sioux: Moon When Horns Are Broken Off

Roman: Ninth Month (from March)

THE WISDOM OF THE DARK SEASON

While September and October tend to be bright with colorful leaves and warm afternoon sun, November brings with it the true, grey grip of the coming winter. The trees are bare now, seeming to shiver in the cold winds, and the snow may have begun falling in most parts of the Northern Hemisphere, where Snow Moon is a common name. This past year in the prairies, we had an unseasonably warm Halloween, and then an ominous day of clouds, and then on November 2nd, a three-day snowstorm blew in and sentenced me to my snow shovel for most of a week. Winter had arrived.

This month's moon has plenty of evocative names, like Frost Moon, Freezing Moon, Dark Moon, and Snow Moon. If you hadn't yet noticed, we're in the waning of the year, and it's time to pay attention to the power of the cold.

One of this month's names is the Beaver Moon. This is the time when the beavers are busiest, preparing their winter shelters. That may have made them easier to trap at this time (and extra valuable with their cozy winter coats on) and the beaver pelt trade was important for both the Indigenous and Colonial Americans for a time—as indicated by the Cherokee name for this lunation, the Trading Moon.

But the beavers also have an important lesson for us as we observe their behavior in the winter. Unlike some mammals, beavers don't hibernate during the winter. They are, indeed, busy, perhaps most of all at this time of the year, but even they are preparing to slow down for the colder months. Part of their work is preparing dams that allow their winter lodges to maintain water that doesn't freeze. They've been busy collecting food stores and getting their homes ready during the harvest season, and then they head inside to mate (beavers: they're just like us!). The coldest part of the winter season is spent inside their lodges gestating and caring for their young.

November is the last month before the winter solstice, when the sun is waning toward its darkest point. Now we must prepare for the stillness of winter and get ready for the embrace of frost and snow. This month can feel heavy, edging toward depression. In Canada, the only statutory holiday in this month is Remembrance Day, a day to consider the losses of those who gave their lives to war. We remain in the season of death after Samhain, but it feels like more of a time to mourn quietly than to party with the ghosts.

Despite the many seasonal clues from September and October, the bare trees and whipping winds of the Frost Moon can come as a bit of a shock. Like the beavers, we should be wrapping up projects and preparing to head inside to rest and make love and eat our winter stores. We tend not to pay too much attention to seasonal shifts, however, and it's rare in this culture to take time off and allow our bodies to transition when the weather changes. Enter cold and flu season—if you do not choose to rest, the body will often choose it for you.

For a long time, I hated November the most. I wanted to escape to some tropical island and stay away until May. To this day, I get sick in some way every single November. Someone once told me that we need to have a cold every fall to reset the pleura in our lungs, a little bit like a snake shedding its summer skin for a hardier winter stock. I don't know if there's any truth to that, but I like the metaphor.

I won't say I enjoy getting sick every November, but I have come to respect this windy, cold, colorless time of year. This lunation can be an initiation into the wisdom of the dark season, a portal through the frost of grief, an invitation to a sort of hibernation that can be generative and sweet, especially when we eventually thaw out again in the spring, ideally refreshed from a long winter's rest.

The dark, frosty winter is a time for learning, for going deeper into our spiritual awareness, into our dreams, our wishes, our shadows, and our intuition. When we take this time to slow down, head inside, and do our winter work, we can help our spirits evolve and heal. Of course, we still live in the material world and we'll do our best to balance these energies with what we need to get done at work, school, and home. But if we can give ourselves a little more permission to slow down, rest, and snuggle into our winter lodges, we might begin to see that November's Frost Moon has its own unique gifts.

SEASONAL WELLNESS

- November is a time of wind and cold in many parts of the Northern Hemisphere. Cover your head and your neck when you go outside and keep yourself warm with hot tea, hot water bottles, and warm baths.

- This lunation is all about wrapping up and letting go. Finish your projects for the year and prepare for rest.

- The waning year is best spent processing and integrating. If possible, take a break from creating and relax into the routines that nourish you the most.

- Sometimes new projects come up at this time anyway. Focus on the gestation part: the thinking, planning, and feeling aspects of the project, and wait to send it out into the world if you can.

- Self-care routines are important all the time, but you may find you have less energy now, so it's helpful to have habits in place you can lean on without having to think too much about them. Be careful that you don't skip meals or rest.

- You may begin to notice a need for more sleep as the nights lengthen. Lean into this if you can by going to bed earlier. Naps are good anytime, but you may find a natural urge to sleep a longer night rather than napping during the day.

- Warm, nourishing food is especially important as our bodies are transitioning from fall to winter. Focus on cooked, spiced food and nourishing, warm bone broths, especially if you have a cold or flu.

JOURNAL PROMPTS

What do I discover when I draw away from the outside world and turn inwards? What is hidden in my shadows? What am I learning, grieving, dreaming, wishing, hoping for?

AFFIRMATION

I trust my intuition and give myself time and space to listen.

THE HIGH PRIESTESS

The High Priestess is often shown sitting between a black and a white pillar in front of a thin veil decorated with pomegranates. Pomegranates link her to the divine feminine, the subconscious mind, and the secrets of intuition. The High Priestess has a crown on her head and a crescent moon at her feet. In the *Modern Witch* tarot deck by Lisa Sterle, she is also holding an open laptop. The High Priestess is one who knows how to sit between the conscious and unconscious worlds. She is fully connected to the world of magic and mystery while also getting her emails done. She is sovereign over both the inner and the outer worlds. The Frost Moon lunation invites us deeper into the dark half of the year, where our work is to look inward, to connect with our intuition, our subconscious, our dreams, and all that is unseen. At the same time, however, we have the practical realities of the world to attend to, and we may need to balance our draw to mystery with the everyday realities of family and work. The High Priestess invites us to pull back the veil, while remembering who we must also be in the conscious, material world.

THE HIGH PRIESTESS

YOGA POSE

SEATED FORWARD BEND

November's Frost Moon is a time to turn inward, slow down, and connect with our intuition. This forward bend is known in Sanskrit as *paschimottanasana*, which means intense western-facing stretch. This is said to be the half of the body that receives, and opening anywhere along this line can trigger a relaxation response.

Sit on the edge of a small cushion or foam yoga block so that your pelvis is slightly tilted forward. Extend your legs straight out in front of you, feet flexed. Your feet can be together or hip-width apart. Your knees can be as bent as you like. Feel free to add a bolster under your knees for extra comfort and ease for a tight lower back.

Sit up tall, then gently fold forward over your legs, aiming your heart beyond your feet rather than your head to your knees. Do not pull. Hold for five to eight breaths. Breathe deeply into your back body, receiving space and breath into this part of your body.

When you are ready to come out, gently lie down on your back. Allow the knees to fall apart so the soles of your feet are together, which will reset your lower back.

TAROT RITUAL

Tarot is a wonderful tool to help tap into your subconscious mind and hone your intuition for November's Frost Moon. Try this simple ritual with a tarot deck.

Light a candle and hold your tarot deck in your hands. Take a moment to remember and acknowledge the land you are on and your relationship with that land.

Imagine a circle of protection around yourself, made of salt, stones, or whatever else resonates with you. Clarify that only loving, healing energies are invited into the circle. Set your intention for what you might want to know from the cards. Ask an open question, such as "What do I need to know to connect with my highest self?"

While meditating on your question, shuffle the cards in whatever way works best for you. When you feel ready, set the deck in front of you and cut it in half with your non-dominant hand. Place the bottom half on top, and then pull three cards from the top.

Place the three cards in order face up. The first one represents the past, or energies you are moving through or away from. The second card represents you in the present, and the third card represents the future, or energies that could play into your future decisions and experiences.

Resist the urge to immediately look up the meanings of the card in your deck's booklet. Instead, pick up each card one at a time and really look at it. What do you notice about the card? How do you tell the story of what you see on the card? And how do you feel when you look at it? If there is a character on the card, do you relate to that character or not? If you could talk to this character, what would you say? How do you imagine they'd respond?

Repeat this process for the other two cards. Feel free to write down your reflections. Once you've completed this, go ahead and look up the card's meanings if you want to and see if they add anything to your reading.

When this ritual feels complete for you, thank the cards, the land, and anything else that you'd like to offer gratitude toward, then blow out the candle.

DIANA: GODDESS OF THE MOON

The Roman goddess Diana, known to the Greeks as Artemis, is a goddess of the hunt and the moon. She is an appropriate deity to think about around the Hunter's Moon of October and November, when the moon rises around sunset, providing more light for predators working at night. Even today, some hunters rely on moonlight to help them track their prey, but this would have been especially vital when hunting was necessary for survival.

Diana is a fierce huntress, preferring the wildness of the woods and her friends the nymphs to the oppressive path of marriage to a man. In one of her most famous stories, Diana was relaxing naked in a pool in the woods with the nymphs. The hunter Actaeon stopped to rest by the cool waters of this pool after a long and successful day of hunting with his dogs, not realizing who else was in the water. Actaeon accidentally caught a glimpse of the naked goddess. Furious, Diana immediately transformed him into a stag and he ran off, pursued by his hunting dogs, who took him down to his death.

This story is often told as an example of Diana's fierce protection over her own sexual agency. It also, however, teaches about the delicate line between hunter and hunted. Most modern people do not need to worry about hunting to live, but there was a time when the wild unknown forces of the woods could make the difference between surviving the winter or not.

Hunting was also a vital practice for the indigenous people of the US and Canada (and everywhere else before we got our meat at the grocery store). In her book *Braiding Sweetgrass*, Robin Wall Kimmerer explains the concept of the Honorable Harvest, an idea that many indigenous societies hold as one of the highest principles of respect for the land. When harvesting certain plants, for example, we should never take more than half, and we should ensure that the parts we don't eat are used for other things or returned to the forest or the animals to be used in another way. The land gives us life and takes care of us, so we must be respectful and give back in return.

Diana is a goddess of liminal places. She presides over the relationship between life and death, between wildness and civilization. She can provide abundance on a moonlit night, or the sharp pang of a hungry nothing when she pulls her light away. She reminds us of the importance of the principles of the Honorable Harvest, to remember ourselves as a part of a wild world that can give as easily as take. Even if hunting is very far away from our everyday realities, how can we remember ourselves as animals that rely on unseen and unknown forces? Can we offer gratitude and respect for our abundance, whatever it might look like today?

DECEMBER

LONG NIGHT MOON

Names of the Moon

Neo–Pagan: Long Night Moon

Mohican: Long Night Moon

Chinese: Bitter Moon

Celtic: Cold Moon

Mohawk: Cold Moon

Cherokee: Snow Moon

Haida: Snow Moon

English Medieval: Oak Moon

Wiccan: Oak Moon

Western Abenaki: Winter Maker Moon

Anishinaabe: Little Spirit Moon

Dakota Sioux: Twelfth Moon

Colonial American: Christmas Moon

European: Moon Before Yule

Roman: Tenth Month (from March)

REST AND REFLECTION

We've made it to the last month of the calendar year, where we greet the winter solstice. This is the longest night of the year, usually around December 21st in the Northern Hemisphere. Where I live in the Canadian prairies, the night lasts about 16 hours. The sun seems to get ready to set around 3:30 pm, and it just barely rises after 8:30 am, spending the day lazily circling the horizon. This lunation is called the Long Night Moon because this full moon will tend to be visible in the sky for longer than at other times of the year, often for several days in a row. The moon will likely feel much more present than the sun around now. This is the peak of Moon Season, the darkest part of the dark half of the year.

This month also has a suite of other names like Cold Moon, Snow Moon, and Winter Maker Moon. This is no joke: where I live, the temperature often drops below –30 degrees Celsius (–22°F), and sometimes when it does you can see the air literally glittering in a ray of sunshine. It's so cold that any droplet of moisture in the air immediately freezes, creating ice crystals that dance and reflect the light of the sun. You can go outside when the air is glittering, but it makes you cough because you're breathing in ice crystals. It's simultaneously beautiful and horrifying.

The winter solstice is a powerful moment in the Wheel of the Year. Even as we hit the absolute nadir of darkness in the year, we know that means the light is about to shift from waning to waxing. From here on out, the light will grow a little bit every day until the summer solstice, where northern climates like mine will receive a full nine and a half more hours of daylight than we're getting right now. Pretty much every world religion and tradition has some kind of celebration oriented around the winter solstice.

This is the solstice, the still point of the sun, its cusp and midnight, the year's threshold and unlocking, where the past lets go of and becomes the future; the place of caught breath, the door of a vanished house left ajar

~ MARGARET ATWOOD, SHAPECHANGERS IN WINTER

Christmas is celebrated on December 25th as the birthday of Jesus Christ. Symbolically, the winter solstice represents the return of the light, the rebirth of the sun/son. Jesus, the Son of God, was killed by the Romans via crucifixion. It was said that he died around 3:00 pm and then the sun went dark for three hours (a solar eclipse?). He was removed from the cross and placed in a tomb, which was discovered to be empty three days later. While Jesus's resurrection is officially celebrated around Easter, this is the story that the sun tells every winter solstice: a moment of death and darkness inevitably leads to new life. In that sense, it is Jesus's symbolic birthday, and a good time for ancient Christians to compete and combine with the popular pagan solstice celebrations of the time, including Germanic Yule celebrations.

Popularly, Christmas is the "most wonderful time of the year." It's meant to be a time of celebrations, love, and gift-giving, and it certainly can be that. But the mood of the winter solstice is a little more somber. It invites us to focus on grief and loss, to reflect on the past year, and to start considering desires and intentions for the next year.

For a few years in a row, I participated in a shared solstice ceremony where we would express our grief, one at a time, through words, movement, sounds, or however else we wanted to express it. When each person had given their offering of grief to the circle, the others would simply say, in unison, "we're with you." Spending time with others honoring the power and importance of grief near this time was incredibly nourishing for me. It's natural to consider grief on the long, dark nights and to want to look back on your year and what worked for you and what didn't. Having a place to ritualize that outside of all the forced cheer of Christmas gave that side of me some space to enjoy the celebratory side of the season a lot more.

Ultimately, the winter solstice is a time for rest. The word "solstice" comes from the Latin *sol*, which means sun and *sistere*, which means stillness. At this time, it appears that the sun rests below the horizon; it pauses in its trajectory across the sky. So do the trees and many of the animals. So should we.

SEASONAL WELLNESS

- Rest. Our bodies literally need more sleep in the darker seasons than in the bright seasons, so go to bed earlier if you can, take naps, and don't try to resist it with too much coffee and artificial light. It's normal to be more tired.

- Work with stillness practices like meditation and Yin or Restorative yoga.

- Continue to nourish your body with warm teas and cooked foods.

- Enjoy the special foods and celebrations of the holiday season, but hydrate and eat with your drinks if you are drinking alcohol. Avoiding sugar on an empty stomach will help keep your blood sugar level, which helps keep your mood level as well.

- Learn the history and meaning of the holiday celebrations in your tradition and attend to the spiritual aspects of those rituals where they resonate with you.

- When possible, maximize time spent with loved ones, and minimize time with those that stress you out.

- Book rest days for yourself, especially if you have a busy holiday season with lots of visiting. If you're traveling, try to return home a day or two early so that you have some rest before you have to go back to work.

- As always, spend time outside if you can, ideally during daylight hours, and notice what the natural world is doing.

- Ritualize the solstice and/or this month's full moon with a focus on grief and loss and setting intentions for the new year, ideally with others.

JOURNAL PROMPTS

What did I learn over this past year? What am I grieving? What do I wish for as the light begins to return and a new year begins?

AFFIRMATION

I am allowed to rest. I am allowed to grieve.

THE HERMIT

The Hermit tarot card usually shows a person in a simple hooded robe, often at the top of a lonely mountain, walking by the light of a small lamp. This is the archetype of the monk or ascetic, the one who escapes from everyday life to do their spiritual practices. This is what our spirit needs around December's Long Night Moon. When this card comes up, we're often already craving a break from our everyday lives, to get quiet, be alone, and rest. The Hermit's lamp only illuminates the very next step, allowing him to focus only on what's right in front of him. This isn't meant to be permanent, for most of us, but rather a necessary pause to allow us to reflect on what's been happening in our lives and how we would like to re-enter it after this spiritual rest.

YOGA POSE

SAVASANA

The word *savasana* in Sanskrit breaks down into *sava*, which means "corpse," and *asana*, which means "pose," so this is Corpse Pose, the yoga posture of death. Traditionally, it is the final posture of any yoga class, the only one that is non-negotiable in a given sequence. Once the practice is finished, we must rest, we must surrender, "die" to what has happened so that we can be reborn again. This is a posture of rest, pause, and release, ideally both physically and emotionally.

Lie down on your back, arms open to your sides, legs splayed out and relaxed. Feel free to add an eye mask, blanket, or pillow under your knees for extra comfort. Once you're comfortable in the pose, take a deep breath to settle in. Allow your body to sink into the earth, and let your mind wander so that you're not focusing on any one particular thing.

Stay anywhere from three to twenty minutes. When you're ready to get up, do so slowly and gently, beginning with deepening your breath and then slowly wiggling your fingers and toes, then press yourself up to sitting position.

You can do this pose at the end of a yoga sequence or on its own. It's a good idea to practice Savasana daily for ten to twenty minutes throughout December and the winter season, as it supports and restores all the systems of the body, especially when you're feeling tired and overwhelmed.

WINTER SOLSTICE RITUAL

This ritual could be done on the winter solstice itself or on the day of December's full moon. All you need is a candle, a pen, and some paper.

Sit with the candle unlit in front of you. Turn off the lights so you are in relative darkness. Take a moment to consider the land that you are on and your relationship with it. Imagine a circle of protection around you made of salt or stones, filtering out any unhelpful energies and only allowing in the energies that are in alignment with your highest good.

List your losses this year. Consider what you are grieving, which can include relationships, aspects of your identity, job changes, and so on. Take some time to grieve, to feel sad, to miss these things. Take at least three deep breaths to allow the feelings of grief to flow through you without trying to change them. Write them down if you like.

When this feels complete for you, consider what you gained this year, including lessons you learned from what changed or was lost. If you are grieving someone, consider what they brought into your life that you get to keep. Take at least three deep breaths to allow any emotions arising here to flow through you. Write these down if you like.

Now light the candle, bringing light back into your life. This time, name what you want in the coming year. What are your hopes and dreams? Don't hold back—wish as big as you want to. Take at least three deep breaths to draw the wishes into your heart and breathe them out. Write down your wishes.

When this feels complete, thank the circle, the land, the four directions, and anything or anyone else that you feel needs gratitude right now. Blow out the candle to signal the end of the ritual. Keep the paper with your wishes on it to hand so you can refer to it as you return to the various rituals of the Wheel of the Year.

BLUE MOON

While a calendar month fluctuates between 28 and 31 days, a full moon cycle is always 29.5 days. That means that every two to three years, there are thirteen moons in a year rather than twelve. Jonathan Carver, a captain who spent time in the North American prairies with the Dakota Sioux, observed that the extra lunation was named the "lost moon." Today, most people consider a blue moon to be when there are two full moons within a calendar month, which is called a monthly blue moon. However, it can also mean the third full moon within a season that has four full moons, which would be called a seasonal blue moon. In any case, these extra moons are rare(ish). That's where we get the phrase "once in a blue moon": it happens, but infrequently.

The Blue Moon, then, is the thirteenth moon of the calendar year. The number thirteen is often considered unlucky, but that's likely because it has a relationship with witchcraft and feminine power. The moon has often been connected with women and feminine energy, partly because of the association of lunar energy with menstruation. In some ancient goddess cults, menstruation was a time of deep connection to the earth, to the goddess, and to feminine magic.

Friday 13th, in particular, was a special day for celebrating and honoring the goddess. Friday is named in English for the Norse Frig or Freya, a goddess of marriage, motherhood, and psychic powers. In many other languages, including the French *vendredi*, Friday is named for the Roman goddess Venus (or the Greek Aphrodite), a goddess of love, fertility, beauty, and sexuality. As Christianity worked to take over from indigenous goddess worshiping faiths, it spread the concept that thirteen was an unlucky number, related to the thirteen figures of the Last Supper, including Judas, who betrayed Jesus and lead to his death. It is said that Jesus died on Friday 13th. These stories helped to undermine the pagan faith, who saw thirteen as the number of the goddess.

A blue moon gives us an extra opportunity to be in the feminine energy of a full moon. This thirteenth moon can give us a chance to consider even more powerfully what we want to release and how we'd like to connect with the divine feminine, which includes sensuality, passion, play, connection, and intuition.

RITUAL FOR A BLUE MOON

The thirteenth full moon is a perfect time to amplify full moon energy, which can help us release and let go. Please gather:

- A candle

- Matches or a lighter

- A fireproof bowl with a bit of water in it

- Extra water (for safety)

- Pen and paper

Sit comfortably and light your candle. Take a moment to cast your circle, imagining salt or stones, a protective circle filtering out any unhelpful energies and only allowing in the energies that are in alignment with your highest good. Take a moment to consider the land that you are on and your relationship with this land.

You may choose to call on a deity, spirit guide, loved one, or other type of energy to help you let go of what no longer serves you.

Close your eyes and take a few deep breaths. Consider what you are ready and willing to let go of in your life. Habits, patterns, people, whatever it's time to release. Think about each thing and why you'd like to let it go.

When you're ready, write down each thing clearly on a small piece of paper. As you resolve to let go, burn the paper carefully over the fireproof bowl and drop it into the water (before it burns you). Repeat this as many times as you need. Add more water to the bowl to snuff out the fire if needed.

When this feels complete, take a moment to thank your protective circle and any energies that were with you in this process. Blow out your candle. Collect the water and ashes into a container and mindfully dispose of them in a safe place. Then take a bath, shower, or simply wash your hands with intention, solidifying your intention to cleanse and release.

BLACK MOON

A black moon is the second new moon within a calendar month or the third new moon in a season with four new moons. Every now and then, February has no full moon at all, its 28 days slipping just between two full moons, and this is also known as a black moon. Yet another definition is when February has no new moon. This only happens about once every nineteen years, so it's even rarer than a blue moon.

Historically, black moons were powerful times for pagan rituals and witchcraft. This would be a time when the new moon energy would be amplified. New moon energy invites us to dive into the inner world, connect with our spiritual selves, and cast spells to manifest what we want in our lives. A black moon would be a powerful time to activate those energies, consider what we want, and put our magic into action. We are invited to connect with divine feminine energy. This could mean a specific goddess or it could also be about inviting the darker energies of intuition, the subconscious mind, the physical body, and spiritual connection. Keep in mind that this isn't about sex or even gender—feminine and masculine energy exist in everyone and everything in balance.

Unlike a blue moon, black moons are invisible in the sky. The lack of light from the moon, however, can make the stars much brighter, especially in places with very little light pollution. Black moons are, symbolically, a time when the everyday illumination of our lives goes dark, which allows us to see deeper, to reveal what's in the background that we normally wouldn't see. It's a good time for making magic.

RITUAL FOR A BLACK MOON

The thirteenth new moon of a calendar year invites us to connect with divine feminine energy. For this ritual, please gather:

- A candle
- A beverage you like in two cups
- A sweet treat with some on an extra plate

Light your candle and set your space. Visualize a circle of protection around you filtering out any unhelpful energies and only allowing in the energies that are in alignment with your highest good. Do your land acknowledgment. Set an intention to connect with the energy of the goddess for your highest good and the good of all.

Now take some time to invite the goddess, whatever that means for you. Every goddess is a manifestation of divine feminine energy, so if you resonate with Diana, Lalita, Chang'e, one of the feminine tarot card characters, or simply the mood of darkness and intuitive power, imagine that. See your version of the divine feminine in all her glory.

Make an offering to this goddess. Share your drink with her and your special treat. Then spend some time with this goddess energy. Talk to her. Listen for any messages she has for you, which may come through as images, sensations, or words.

When this feels complete for you, thank the goddess, the circle, the land, and any other energies or beings that may have helped in this process. Blow out your candle. Then bring the treats to a special place outside as an offering for the goddess, and leave them overnight. Say a prayer of thanks, and retrieve them in the morning.

BIRTHDAY MOONS

Every now and then, a full moon, new moon, or even an eclipse will fall on the date of your birth. This is an important opportunity to consider what this means for you in the evolution of your own life. Here are some ideas to sit with.

BIRTHDAY FULL MOON

If a full moon falls on your birthday, a certain cycle of your life is complete. It's time to look back at where you've been and what you've been doing in your life thus far. There may be some things you need to let go of or stop doing and allow your life to take a different path.

BIRTHDAY NEW MOON

If your birthday falls on a new moon, you are on the cusp of a new beginning. It's time to receive change in your life and invite those energies that you want to bring in as you enter into the next year of your life. This is a powerful time for setting intentions, so think about what you really want to invite into your life in the coming year.

BIRTHDAY ECLIPSES

Eclipse energy amplifies the energy of the full or new moon. It is also an indication of a major shift in energy in your life. Big changes may be coming for you (or may have already been happening), and though they may feel intense, they can help you in your healing and evolution, especially if you can stay present with what you want and let go of the things that aren't working for you. Reflect on your life so far and what your goals are over the next year, five years, or even ten years. You are being asked to take part in your own evolution.

BIRTHDAY RITUALS

Birthdays can be weird, for some of us. They are meant to be a fun celebration, but they naturally bring a mood of reflection that sometimes feels more melancholy than celebratory. Taking some time out just for you can be an excellent way to connect with yourself and align with your goals on your birthday. Here are some ways to do that.

- Take yourself out for breakfast or a special coffee and write yourself a letter, reflecting on the last year and thinking about what you hope for in the coming year. If you make this a habit, you'll be able to read the previous year's letters and reflect on the evolution of your life through the lens of your birthdays.

- Go for a walk in nature and talk to the trees about how you're reflecting on another year gone by.

- Make a spell jar (as we did in January) and keep it somewhere you can see it often to remind yourself of your intentions for the year ahead.

- Pull a tarot card for your year ahead. You could also pull three cards for the past, present, and future, or twelve cards, one for each of the months ahead. If you don't yet have a deck, buy yourself one you love for your birthday.

- Celebrate yourself and your life path so far, but take some time out to reflect seriously on where you are going and what you really want.

WHEEL OF THE YEAR YOGA SEQUENCE

Here is the full sequence for the Wheel of the Year that you can practice anytime. This sequence is appropriate for most people, but listen to your body. None of this should cause any pain, and check with a practitioner before you try it if you have any questions or concerns. Take a look back at each month for a full description of each pose.

- Child's Pose for January /
  Wolf Moon

- Sun Salutation for February /
  Budding Moon

- Warrior One for March /
  Worm Moon

- Goddess Warrior for April /
  Awakening Moon

- Goddess Pose for May /
  Flower Moon

- Breathe for June /
  Strawberry Moon

- Gate Pose for July /
  Mead Moon

- Melting Heart Pose for August /
  Dog Days' Moon

- Seated Twist for September /
  Harvest Moon

- Pigeon Pose for October /
  Hunter's Moon

- Seated Forward Bend for November /
  Frost Moon

- Savasana for December /
  Long Night Moon

MOON SALUTATION

This is a wonderful sequence that moves the body in most of its directions, much like the Sun Salutation. However, where the Sun Salutation tends to be energizing, the Moon Salutation is a little more calming, so it's a great sequence to do before bed or when you need to wind down. The sequence mirrors the circularity of the moon, the phases from full to new and back again, reaching high to the sky and then getting low toward the earth. Move through this sequence one breath at a time, going at your own pace, which is calming for the nervous system. As always, stop if you feel any pain; this sequence can be a bit hard on the knees, so don't push it if your knees are sensitive.

Stand near the top of your mat facing the long edge so that your mat stretches out to your right.

Inhale: Vajra Mudra: reach your arms up to the sky and interlace them, pointing the first finger up to the sky (like a pretend finger gun).

Exhale: Side Bend toward the mat.

Inhale: Come back to the center.

Exhale: Side Bend away from your mat.

Inhale: Return to the center.

Exhale: Step your right foot out on your mat and turn your toes out.

Inhale: Reach your arms up to the sky in a transition called Star Pose.

Exhale: Goddess Pose: bend your knees out to the sides as you bend your elbows into a cactus shape.

Inhale: Return through Star pose, then turn your right toes out toward the short edge of your mat, turning your left toes in slightly.

Exhale: Triangle Pose: tip your hips back slightly, keeping your legs straight but without locking your right knee. Reach forward and then gently place your right fingertips on your shin, reaching your left arm up to the sky. Lean your chest back gently so that it's in line with your leg.

Inhale in this position.

Exhale: Pyramid Pose: step your back foot in slightly and widen it toward the long edge of your mat. Turn the back foot toward the top of your mat and place your hands gently to either side of your front foot, on blocks if you wish.

Inhale: Lengthen your spine parallel to the ground.

Exhale: Fold over your leg.

Inhale: Look forward.

Exhale: Low Lunge: place your back knee down on the ground, ensuring your front knee is over your ankle.

Inhale: Reach your arms up toward the sky.

Exhale: Half Squat on right leg: return your hands to the ground again and come all the way onto the ball of your right foot so your heel lifts. Allow your left leg to straighten and come onto the heel.

Inhale: If you feel balanced enough, gently bring your hands to your heart.

Exhale: Full Squat: bring your feet in about hip-width or a bit wider and allow the toes to turn out. Settle your hips all the way down to the earth and bring your hands together in front of your heart. Take a full cycle of breath here, in and out.

Inhale: Stay here.

Exhale: Half squat on left leg.

Inhale: Bring your hands to your heart.

Exhale: Low Lunge: turn to the left side of your mat and place your right knee on the ground.

Inhale: Reach your arms up to the sky.

Exhale: Bring your hands to the ground and prepare for Pyramid Pose, stepping your back foot in slightly.

Inhale: Lengthen your chest

Exhale: Fold over your leg.

Inhale: Triangle Pose: reach your right arm up to the sky.

Exhale here.

Inhale: Star Pose: reach your arms up and turn your toes out.

Exhale: Goddess Pose.

Inhale: Straighten your arms and legs.

Exhale: Step toward the right edge of the mat, so the mat is out on your left (the opposite end from where you started) and your feet are parallel, hip-width apart.

Inhale: Vajra Mudra: raise your arms up to the sky.

Exhale: Side Bend toward your mat. Inhale through center. Exhale and Side Bend away from your mat. Inhale back up to center.

Exhale: Step your left foot out onto your mat.

Inhale: Star Pose.

Exhale: Goddess Pose.

Inhale: Straighten the legs and turn the left toes to the left, right toes turn in a little bit.

Exhale: Triangle Pose. Inhale here.

Exhale: Pyramid Pose, stepping your back foot in slightly. Inhale here.

Exhale: To prepare for Low Lunge, place your back foot on the ground.

Inhale: Reach your arms up to the sky.

Exhale: Half Squat: lean your weight onto the ball of your left foot so that your heel lifts and your right legs extends out straight to the right.

Inhale: bring your hands together at your heart.

Exhale: Full Squat. Full inhale and exhale here.

Inhale: Then exhale into Half Squat on the right foot.

Inhale: bring your hands together at your heart.

Exhale: Prepare for Low Lunge with your right leg in front, left knee to the ground.

Inhale: Reach your arms up to the sky.

Exhale: Release your hands to the ground and step your back foot in a bit, preparing for Pyramid Pose.

Inhale: Lengthen your spine.

Exhale: Fold over your leg.

Inhale: Triangle Pose: reach your left arm up to the sky. Stay as you exhale.

Inhale: Star Pose.

Exhale: Goddess Pose.

Inhale: Step back up to the left side of your mat where you started the sequence, reaching your arms up to the sky into Vajra Mudra.

Exhale: Side Bend toward your mat. Inhale through center. Exhale and Side Bend away from your mat. Inhale back up to center.

Inhale: Bring your hands gently together in front of your heart. Breathe normally and take a few moments to simply notice how you feel.

RESOURCES

Find out about the indigenous history and traditional names of your local area (especially for the U.S. and Canada) at: https://native-land.ca/

The Old Farmer's Almanac is an annual resource from the U.S. for weather, moon cycles, and more that has been in print since 1792. You can get the printed version each year, but they also have an excellent website with lots of searchable information here: https://www.almanac.com/

NASA has a detailed section on its website for anyone wanting more details about the science of the moon: https://moon.nasa.gov/

Extract from *Letters I Didn't Write* by John MacKenzie (Nightwood Editions, 2008), used with kind permission.

Braiding Sweetgrass: Indigenous Wisdom, Scientific Knowledge, and the Teachings of Plants by Robin Wall Kimmerer, 2013.

Secrets of the Eternal Moon Phase Goddesses: Meditations on Desire, Relationships and the Art of Being Broken by Julie Peters, SkyLight Paths Publishing, 2016.

ABOUT THE AUTHOR

Julie Peters is a counselor, tarot reader, and yoga teacher working on Plains Cree land in Treaty 6 Territory, also known as Edmonton, Alberta. She is the author of *Secrets of the Eternal Moon Phase Goddesses: Meditations on Desire, Relationships, and the Art of Being Broken* and the Canada Book award-winning *Want: 8 Steps to Recovering Desire, Passion, and Pleasure After Sexual Assault*. She is also a staff writer for *Spirituality and Health Magazine*.

Learn more about her at juliepeters.ca or on Instagram at @juliepeterswellness.

INDEX

THANKS

Thank you first of all to Lizzie Kaye, who found my writing and gave me the opportunity to write this joy of a book. Clare Ashton had so much patience with me through all her thoughtful and thorough edits, and Lauren Spooner did an incredible job bringing these ideas to life through her illustrations. The whole team at David & Charles has been amazing. Thanks as always to my agent, Robert Lecker, who is a massive support and always pushes me to be a better writer. I'm also grateful to Karen Goodfellow, who consulted on this book and offered very wise suggestions.

I'd also like to thank my eternally supportive husband, Robert Beal, and my kiddo, Grant, who quietly watched his shows beside me early in the morning, which is when I wrote most of this book. Finally, deep gratitude for my dog, Finnegan, who got me out looking at the moon in all types of weather. I miss you, buddy.

A DAVID AND CHARLES BOOK
© David and Charles, Ltd 2023

David and Charles is an imprint of David and Charles, Ltd
Suite A, Tourism House, Pynes Hill, Exeter, EX2 5WS

Text © Julie Peters 2023
Layout and Illustrations © David and Charles, Ltd 2023

First published in the UK and USA in 2023

Julie Peters has asserted her right to be identified as author of this work in accordance with the Copyright, Designs and Patents Act, 1988.

A catalogue record for this book is available from the British Library.

ISBN-13: 9781446310632 paperback
ISBN-13: 9781446312179 EPUB
ISBN-13: 9781446312186 PDF

This book has been printed on paper from approved suppliers and made from pulp from sustainable sources.

MIX
Paper from responsible sources
FSC® C012521

Printed in China through Asia Pacific Offset for:
David and Charles, Ltd
Suite A, Tourism House, Pynes Hill, Exeter, EX2 5WS

10 9 8 7 6 5 4 3 2 1

Publishing Director: Ame Verso
Senior Commissioning Editor: Lizzie Kaye
Managing Editor: Jeni Chown
Editor: Jessica Cropper
Project Editor: Clare Ashton
Head of Design: Anna Wade
Designers: Sam Staddon, Jess Pearson and Lee-May Lim
Pre-press Designer: Susan Reansbury
Illustrations: Lauren Spooner
Production Manager: Beverley Richardson

David and Charles publishes high-quality books on a wide range of subjects. For more information visit www.davidandcharles.com.

Follow us on Instagram by searching for @dandcbooks_wellbeing.

Layout of the digital edition of this book may vary depending on reader hardware and display settings.